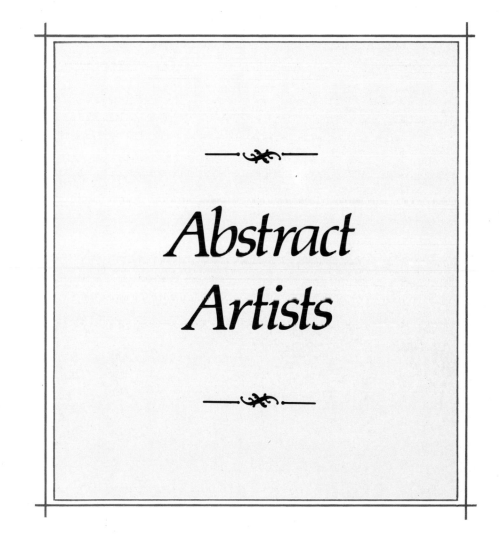

Abstract Artists

GREAT ARTISTS OF THE WESTERN WORLD

Abstract Artists

Wassily Kandinsky

❦

Kasimir Malevich

❦

Joan Miró

❦

Bridget Riley

MARSHALL CAVENDISH · LONDON · NEW YORK · SYDNEY

Staff Credits

Editors	Clive Gregory LLB Sue Lyon BA (Honours)	**Picture Researchers**	Vanessa Fletcher BA (Honours) Flavia Howard BA (Honours) Jessica Johnson BA
Art Editors	Chris Legee BFA Kate Sprawson BA (Honours) Keith Vollans LSIAD	**Production Controllers**	Tom Helsby Alan Stewart BSc
Deputy Editor	John Kirkwood BSc (Honours)	**Secretary**	Lynn Smail
Sub-editors	Caroline Bugler BA (Honours), MA Sue Churchill BA (Honours) Alison Cole BA, MPhil Jenny Mohammadi Nigel Rodgers BA (Honours), MA Penny Smith Will Steeds BA (Honours), MA	**Editorial Director**	Maggi McCormick
		Publishing Manager	Robert Paulley BSc
		Managing Editor	Alan Ross BA (Honours)
Designers	Stuart John Julie Stanniland	**Consultant and Authenticator**	Sharon Fermor BA (Honours) Lecturer in the Extra-Mural Department of London University and Lecturer in Art History at Sussex University

Reference Edition Published 1988

Published by Marshall Cavendish Corporation
147 West Merrick Road
Freeport, Long Island
N.Y. 11520

Typeset by Litho Link Ltd., Welshpool
Printed and Bound by Dai Nippon
Printing Co., Hong Kong Ltd.

Library of Congress Cataloging-in-Publication Data

Main entry under title:

Great Artists of the Western World II.

Includes index.
1. Artists – Biography. I. Marshall Cavendish Corporation.
N40.G774 1988   709'.2'2 [B]   88–4317
ISBN 0–86307–900–8 (set)

ISBN 0–86307–900–8 (set)
      0–86307–760–9 (vol)

Preface

Looking at pictures can be one of the greatest pleasures that life has to offer. Note, however, those two words 'can be'; all too many of us remember all too clearly those grim afternoons of childhood when we were dragged, bored to tears and complaining bitterly, through room after room of Italian primitives by well-meaning relations or tight-lipped teachers. It was enough to put one off pictures for life – which, for some of us, was exactly what it did.

For if gallery-going is to be the fun it should be, certain conditions must be fulfilled. First, the pictures we are to see must be good pictures. Not necessarily great pictures – even a few of these can be daunting, while too many at a time may prove dangerously indigestible. But they must be well-painted, by good artists who know precisely both the effect they want to achieve and how best to achieve it. Second, we must limit ourselves as to quantity. Three rooms – four at the most – of the average gallery are more than enough for one day, and for best results we should always leave while we are still fresh, well before satiety sets in. Now I am well aware that this is a counsel of perfection: sometimes, in the case of a visiting exhibition or, perhaps, when we are in a foreign city with only a day to spare, we shall have no choice but to grit our teeth and stagger on to the end. But we shall not enjoy ourselves quite so much, nor will the pictures remain so long or so clearly in our memory.

The third condition is all-important: we must know something about the painters whose work we are looking at. And this is where this magnificent series of volumes – one of which you now hold in your hands – can make all the difference. No painting is an island: it must, if it is to be worth a moment's attention, express something of the personality of its painter. And that painter, however individual a genius, cannot but reflect the country, style and period, together with the views and attitudes of the people among whom he or she was born and bred. Even a superficial understanding of these things will illuminate a painting for us far better than any number of spotlights, and if in addition we have learnt something about the artist as a person – life and loves, character and beliefs, friends and patrons, and the places to which he or she travelled – the interest and pleasure that the work will give us will be multiplied a hundredfold.

Great Artists of the Western World will provide you with just such an insight into the life and work of some of the outstanding painters of Europe and America. The text is informative without ever becoming dry or academic, not limiting itself to the usual potted biographies but forever branching out into the contemporary world outside and beyond workshop or studio. The illustrations, in colour throughout, have been dispensed in almost reckless profusion. For those who, like me, revel in playing the Attribution Game – the object of which is to guess the painter of each picture before allowing one's eye to drop to the label – the little sections on 'Trademarks' are a particularly happy feature; but every aficionado will have particular preferences, and I doubt whether there is an art historian alive, however distinguished, who would not find some fascinating nugget of previously unknown information among the pages that follow.

This series, however, is not intended for art historians. It is designed for ordinary people like you and me – and for our older children – who are fully aware that the art galleries of the world constitute a virtually bottomless mine of potential enjoyment, and who are determined to extract as much benefit and advantage from it as they possibly can. All the volumes in this collection will enable us to do just that, expanding our knowledge not only of art itself but also of history, religion, mythology, philosophy, fashion, interior decoration, social customs and a thousand other subjects as well. So let us not simply leave them around, flipping idly through a few of their pages once in a while. Let us read them as they deserve to be read – and welcome a new dimension in our lives.

John Julius Norwich is a writer and broadcaster who has written histories of Venice and of Norman Sicily as well as several works on history, art and architecture. He has also made over twenty documentary films for television, including the recent Treasure Houses of Britain series which was widely acclaimed after repeated showings in the United States.

Lord Norwich is Chairman of the Venice in Peril Fund, and member of the Executive Committee of the British National Trust, an independently funded body established for the protection of places of historic interest and natural beauty.

John Julius Norwich

Contents

Introduction

One of the most remarkable features about abstract art is the breadth and variety of its development. Each of the artists in this volume approached abstraction from a markedly different direction and the distinctiveness of their work illustrates the immense scope which non-representational art offers both for experiment and for calculated effect.

The Music of Abstraction

In the case of Kandinsky, the crucial impetus came from the city of Munich which, in the early years of the 20th century, was a melting pot for the latest Symbolist, Expressionist and Jugendstil trends. The common factor uniting these three movements was a desire to escape the shackles of naturalism.

The principal forum for this synthesis was the Blaue Reiter group, which Kandinsky helped to found after the rejection of his semi-abstract Composition V had obliged him to withdraw from the New Artists' Association. The eclectic vision and supreme tolerance of the Blaue Reiter circle made it the ideal testing ground for his new theories.

Nevertheless, Kandinsky edged cautiously towards abstraction. Despite their non-objective titles ('Compositions', 'Improvisations', etc.), many of his pre-war paintings included recognizable figurative elements (for example, pp.24-5 and 27) or dealt with representational themes (such as the depiction of conflict in Composition IV, p.21). Even in those paintings where he abandoned natural forms, Kandinsky was still using his canvases as a means of portraying a significant human reality.

Kandinsky was here reflecting the mystical symbolism which lay at the heart of the Blaue Reiter. His close friend, Franz Marc, had evolved a complex coding system for each of the colours (blue symbolizing spirituality; yellow, sensuality; red, materialism, and so on), and Kandinsky extended this to the various geometric forms which he used in his pictures, endowing them with different spiritual qualities. Abstraction, therefore, provided for him a new means to an old goal since, by restricting himself to 'non-material' forms, he hoped to approach more directly the spiritual core of art.

In presenting his arguments, Kandinsky made frequent reference to the analogies between music and painting. Thus, in alluding to the importance of colour in echoing the 'inner resonance' of a picture, he declared that 'colour is the keyboard, the eyes are the hammers, the soul is the piano with many strings'. This desire to create 'musical' paintings had been a central feature of the Symbolist movement and it was to become a linking factor between many of the abstract artists. Bridget Riley, for example, retained the musical comparisons in some of her works (for example, pp. 118-19).

Kandinsky's own style altered dramatically in the latter part of his career. During his years at the Bauhaus, he adopted a hard-edged, ordered approach which owed much to the example of Paul Klee, his former colleague in the Blaue Reiter. In the intervening years, between his two spells in Germany, Kandinsky spent a comparatively barren period in his native Russia. These years were, by contrast, the most productive of Malevich's career,

The artists
(clockwise from top) Kandinsky in 1905; Malevich in about 1924; Riley in the mid-1960s; Miró in his eighties.

even though he was later to encounter similar problems to those affecting his fellow countryman.

The New Order of Suprematism

Despite their shared nationality, however, Kandinsky and Malevich were responding to different traditions. The former, by virtue of his time in Munich, developed out of the German Expressionist movement, whereas Malevich was drawn to abstraction through the Cubo-Futurist style that was popular in Russian avant-garde circles before World War One.

Malevich deliberately chose the rectangle as the principal component of his Suprematist pictures because it was a man-made, anti-natural form. Initially, he also restricted his palette to red, white and black, in a further attempt to impose a new order upon nature. This self-restraint has been used as a stylistic device by a number of abstract artists. Echoes of it can be found in the Neo-Plasticism of Mondrian, and in Bridget Riley's early work, where she painted solely in black and white.

Malevich's Suprematist movement evolved alongside that of the Constructivist school, led by Tatlin. Formally, the two styles had much in common, but they differed radically in their philosophies. Constructivism, in essence, was a functional movement which sought to harness art to the needs of society, while Suprematism was an aesthetic trend, dedicated to the painting of 'pure sensation'. Malevich was anxious to place his discoveries at the service of the Revolution, but his metaphysical theories were too rarefied to be of practical use to the new socialist regime. 'At the

The circle
(below) Kandinsky attached great importance to the circle, which he saw as a perfect synthesis of contrasts – that is, between concentric and eccentric movements. Composition VIII *(1923) illustrates this variability: the circles range from the 'quiet' white circle at the top right to the 'noisy' forms which can be seen at the top left-hand corner.*

present moment, man's path lies through space', he wrote. 'Suprematism is the semaphore of colour in this endlessness.' These words were written in 1919, the year in which Malevich officially announced the death of the movement.

During the 1920s, the vanguard of abstraction shifted away from Russia. Malevich had reached an impasse after his series of 'White' paintings (p.67), the Constructivists were increasingly drawn away from painting into utilitarian projects such as industrial design, and the political authorities were keener, in any case, to promote socialist realism as the source of artistic expression. As a result, the mainstream of abstract art developed elsewhere, through the De Stijl movement in Holland and through the Bauhaus in Germany, both of which were indebted to Constructivism.

Controlled Abstraction
There was, however, an alternative tradition which flourished separately in France, as a part of the Surrealist movement, and it was this trend which Miró exploited after his arrival in Paris. The Surrealists endeavoured to produce art that reflected the workings of the unconscious and, to this end, they made use of automatic drawings and images that were obtained without rational intervention, either through trances or dreams.

Miró approved of the methods, if not the aims, of the Surrealists and, accordingly, he used the hallucinations which he suffered as a result of hunger as the source of inspiration for a number of works (see pp.88-9). However, the chance creation of these forms provided only an initial stimulus for the artist and Miró was in full control of the finished result.

In this way, Miró reversed the approach which had been adopted by many of the earlier abstract painters. For, where most of his predecessors had started with a natural form or an idea and progressed from this towards an abstract image, Miró frequently began his paintings with a series of non-objective shapes and worked backwards from them towards a figurative subject (for example, see works on pp. 92-3).

Ironically, Miró's most abstract paintings appeared towards the end of his career, as a painterly lyricism replaced some of his whimsicality (see pp. 96-7). In a late interview, he declared that 'Little by little, I reached the point of not using more than a small number of forms and colours. It is not the first time that painting has been done with a very reduced range of colours. The 10th-century frescoes were painted in the same way.'

Form versus Colour
A similar economy of means is also evident in the work of Bridget Riley although, in her case, there was no question of reanimating an ancient tradition. Rather, she discovered that the greatest pictorial effects were achieved by allowing either form or colour to predominate. 'Form and colour seem to be fundamentally incompatible . . .', she has said. 'When I was developing complex forms, the energies of the medium could only be fully released by simplifying colour . . . Conversely, colour energies need a virtually neutral vehicle if they are to develop uninhibited.' In practice, this meant that when she introduced colour into her paintings, she found it necessary to abandon the elaborate patterns of her black and white pictures and reduce the compositional format to simple stripes (pp.130-31).

In the short term, the Op Art style pioneered by Riley grew out of the pure design and hard-edged abstraction favoured by the Bauhaus and De Stijl and, in particular, out of the experiments of Albers and Vasarély. Ultimately, however, Riley owed a greater debt to two older movements: the Neo-Impressionism of Seurat and Italian Futurism. From the former, she derived the theories of optical mixture, relating to the vibrancy of colours, while, from the latter, she drew the essence of her subject-matter, movement itself.

Riley's approach to movement has undergone startling changes. In early pictures like Blaze I and Shiver (pp.120 and 121), the effects were aggressive and the spectator's eye travels over them uneasily, searching in vain for stability and equilibrium. By contrast, her later paintings are calming and hypnotic, and have frequently been compared to the rhythmic motion of water.

In spite of the recurrent claims about its imminent demise, abstract painting has remained a dominant force in modern art and most of the trends described above have continued to evolve. The automatism of the Surrealists paved the way for the Abstract Expressionists and their French counterparts, the Tachistes; Hard-Edged Abstraction developed into Post-Painterly Abstraction; and the visual trickery of Op Art has found a successor in Abstract Illusionism.

WASSILY KANDINSKY

1866-1944

Kandinsky was one of the first and most important abstract painters of this century. He only began to paint at the age of 30 and invented a new language of forms to express his inner spiritual visions which were based on simplified natural objects and, later, on geometrical figures. His training as a law student helped him formulate his theories of abstract painting in a series of articles and books.

He had tremendous energy, travelling extensively, involving himself in art movements, painting and writing all the while. Returning to Russia after the Revolution, he was on cultural committees setting up new museums, but left when the State began to dictate what art was. Throughout many difficult periods, he continued to refine and perfect the abstract language which altered the course of 20th-century art.

A Modern Experimenter

A Muscovite, whose life and art were haunted by the atmosphere of his birthplace, Kandinsky was indefatigable in his development of a new abstract art and in his endeavours as an arts administrator.

The young Kandinsky
(below) This photograph shows Kandinsky at about the age of five or six, at the time of the family's move from Moscow to Odessa. From an early age he proved to be an unusually bright child, revealing a talent for music, drawing and painting.

Wassily Kandinsky was born in Moscow on 4 December 1866. His father was a prosperous tea merchant whose family had originated from Siberia, from where they had been exiled for failing to provide one of the Russian Grand Dukes with fresh horses for his travels. His mother, Lydia Ticheef, was a beautiful Muscovite whom Kandinsky remembered as 'golden-haired Mother Moscow' because, like the city itself, she had a calm perfection and radiance which masked her nervous energy.

Kandinsky spent his early childhood in Moscow and the colourful city left a lasting impression on his mind. He loved its cathedrals and palaces, the golden cupolas and the bells ringing out from the churches. The colours and atmosphere of Moscow haunted his imagination, and he later fondly recalled its landmarks: 'The hard red, unshakable and silent ring of the Kremlin walls' and 'the slender-white, gracefully devout and serious bell tower of Ivan the Great'.

In 1871, the family moved to Odessa in the Ukraine, and soon after, his parents divorced. Kandinsky's aunt, Elisabeth Ticheef, took his education in hand and instilled in him a love of the strange native folklore and the various fairytales which she and his grandmother would relate. Kandinsky did well in drawing and painting at school and when he was ten years old, his father found him a drawing master. However, he

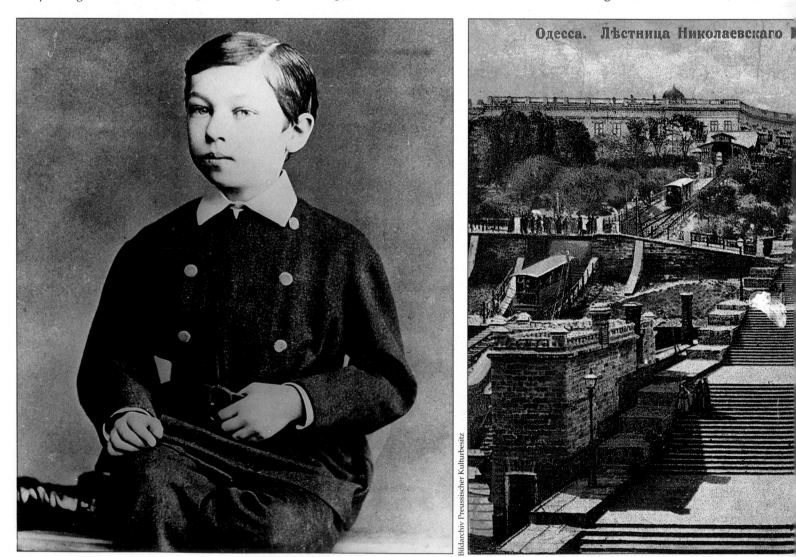

Одесса. Лѣстница Николаевскаго

Well-to-do parents
(right) These photographs of Kandinsky's parents were probably taken in the year of his birth. His father was a wealthy tea-merchant who would later provide his son with a generous private income, while his mother was a beautiful and cultured Muscovite.

Childhood in Odessa
(below) In 1871, the Kandinsky family moved to the picturesque seaport of Odessa in the Ukraine. Soon after their arrival, Kandinsky's parents were divorced and his aunt, Elisabeth, saw him through high school, ensuring that he received a good classical education.

Gabriele Münter-Johannes Eichner-Stiftung

Gabriele Münter-Johannes Eichner-Stiftung

pa.

Jean-Loup Charmet

eventually decided on a more acceptable professional career in law and proved to be an exceptionally bright student. In 1892, he graduated from Moscow University and was immediately offered a teaching appointment at the Law School.

At the back of his mind, however, Kandinsky always felt that in art he would perhaps find more fulfilment than in the mental discipline of his law studies. In 1896, he refused a Professorship at the University of Dorpat in Estonia, and gave up law to become the manager of a printing firm.

THE IMPACT OF MONET

In the year before, an exhibition of French Impressionist painting came to Moscow, and Kandinsky was overwhelmed by one of Monet's *Haystacks* paintings. Prior to this, he had only known the sentimental and narrative paintings of the Russian school. Quite ignorant of the Impressionist style, he could barely recognize the subject of Monet's picture, but it revealed to him the dramatic and expressive power of pure colour.

This event proved to be the inspiration Kandinsky needed and in 1896, aged 30, he took the momentous decision to commit himself totally to painting. 'The drudgery is behind me' he declared, 'before me lies the kind of work I like.' He packed up and set off to study in Munich, then a thriving artistic centre where many other expatriate Russian intellectuals and painters had congregated. His cousin, Anja Chimiakin, whom he had married in 1892, accompanied him, but their marriage was not destined to last.

Munich brought alive for Kandinsky the romance of the Middle Ages and of his childhood fairytales. Initially, there were no financial worries

Städt. Galerie im Lenbachhaus, München

Pupil and mistress
(above) In 1901, Kandinsky formed the Phalanx group of artists. This snapshot shows him (on the far left) with his pupils during a holiday in the Bavarian Alps. His mistress, Gabriele Münter, is standing next to him.

for Kandinsky's father generously provided a private income which allowed the couple to live very well in the Schwabing, Munich's bohemian quarter. Kandinsky joined Anton Azbe's school, then the most popular school in the city. However, he soon tired of studying anatomy, and would skip classes to paint from memory at home, or to sketch scenes in the old Schwabing.

In an attempt to discipline his drawing, Kandinksy enrolled in Franz von Stuck's class at the Munich Royal Academy, but Stuck despaired of his strident colours and exaggerated effects. At Stuck's he met Paul Klee who was later to become a very close friend, and who recalled of their student days: 'Kandinsky was quiet and used to mix his colours on the palette with the greatest diligence and, it seemed to me, with a kind of scholarliness . . .'

Many friends described Kandinsky as a reserved man with an aristocratic and scholarly air, and his studios were always quite unlike those of most other painters: orderly, not to say fastidious, with all the paints and bottles lined up in strict little rows, shoulder-to-shoulder on the shelves. He never had a spot of paint on him while working on a canvas, and used to joke that he could paint in evening dress.

Despite his natural reserve, Kandinsky had

The Influence of Schönberg

Kandinsky first heard Arnold Schönberg's music at a concert in 1911. Immediately inspired, he wrote to the composer and their meeting later that year was the beginning of a close friendship. The two men found they shared the same ideals, both of them breaking time-honoured rules of composition in their own fields. Kandinsky was also an enthusiastic and sensitive amateur musician, while Schönberg painted in his spare time. Kandinsky was encouraged by Schönberg's belief that a musical composition need not adhere to a particular key, equating the composer's revolutionary 'atonality' with his own development towards abstraction.

Arnold Schönberg
(left) The inscription reads: 'Dear Mr Kandinsky, I free myself in notes from an obligation which I would have liked to fulfil long ago.'

Impression 3 (Concert)
(right) Kandinsky's impression of a concert shows the heads of the audience and a grand piano like a black triangle.

'The Blue Rider'
*(left) In 1911, Kandinsky,
together with the painter,
Franz Marc, founded a
new artistic group in
Munich, called* Der Blaue
Reiter *('The Blue Rider'),
dedicated to encouraging a
variety of artistic styles,
including abstract
painting. The group's
Almanac was published
in the following year.*

Nina Kandinsky
*(right) After the
breakdown of his first
marriage, and following
the cooling of his long
affair with Gabriele
Münter, Kandinsky
married Nina Andreewsky
in Moscow in 1917. Nina
was a young and beautiful
woman, and their
marriage was a happy
one, lasting until
Kandinsky's death in
December 1944.*

Bildarchiv Preussischer Kulturbesitz

great administrative skills and enjoyed working
with people. In Munich, he devoted much time
and energy to organizing associations of artists and
exhibitions. The first was the Phalanx group
formed in 1901, which became a forum for the
avant-garde artists of the *Jugendstil* – the German
equivalent of Art Nouveau. Here he met Gabriele
Münter in 1902, and she became first his pupil
and then his mistress, following the breakdown
of his marriage.

Thanks to his private income, Kandinsky had
no urgent need to sell his work, so he was free to
experiment and to indulge his passion for travel, in
order to discover what was happening in other
European artistic centres. He and Gabriele would
disappear for months on end to Italy, France,
Switzerland and even Africa, although he never
took her back to Russia, and in 1906-7 they spent a
year living outside Paris at Sèvres.

BREAKTHROUGH INTO COLOUR

In 1908, Kandinsky and Gabriele moved into a
spacious apartment on the Ainmillerstrasse in
Munich. They also bought a house in Murnau, a
picturesque market town on the Staffelsee in
Upper Bavaria where the Russian painter, Alexei
von Jawlensky, joined them. Having studied with
Matisse, Jawlensky encouraged Kandinsky to
depict the surrounding landscape in broad,
simplified masses, using the brilliant luminous
colours of the Fauves.

This was a major breakthrough. Back in
Munich, Kandinsky concentrated on reworking
the same few motifs, simplifying and abstracting
them so that line and colour, rather than the
objects themselves, became the vehicles for the
expression of his emotions and sensations. One
day, returning to his studio at dusk, he was
overcome by the breathtaking beauty and glow
of a painting of no recognizable subject.
Approaching it, he realized that it was one of his
own, standing on its side against the wall. In that
moment, he understood that the realistic depiction
of ordinary objects was no longer of importance to
his own work.

Kandinsky's new development towards
abstraction dismayed the Munich critics and even
some of his own friends. After a bitter row, he left
the *Neue Künstlervereinigung München* – a group he
had chaired himself – and in 1911, formed *Der
Blaue Reiter* ('The Blue Rider') group with Franz
Marc. Their two exhibitions in 1911 and 1912 were
designed to show 'by a variety of forms the
manifold ways in which the artist manifests his
inner desire'. All styles were represented, from the
abstract paintings of Kandinsky himself to the
naïve art of 'le Douanier' Rousseau. Amongst the
exhibitors was the composer, Arnold Schönberg,
who painted as a hobby.

Like Kandinsky, Schönberg was challenging
the conventional ideas of composition, and the
two men became close friends. Kandinsky himself
had a keen understanding and love of music and,

Städt. Galerie im Lenbachhaus, München

Arthotek/© ADAGP 1988

spiritual rejuvenation through the arts were shattered when the Communist government clamped down on the Russian avant-garde, demanding that henceforth all art should be for the proletariat – cheap art for the streets, for factories and for the houses of workers. Kandinsky felt completely alienated in this atmosphere.

In 1924, the Institute of Artistic Culture was closed down, but the avant-garde had long since dispersed. Kandinsky had returned to Germany in 1921, hoping to live off the proceeds from the sale of 150 pictures he had left at the Der Sturm Gallery. But they had sold for a song. With the drastic depreciation of the German mark, Kandinsky found himself poverty stricken. He had lost two close friends in the war – Franz Marc and August Macke – and the outlook was depressing. However his old friend, Klee, succeeded in finding

Summer days
(above) Taken during his time at the Bauhaus, this photograph shows the Kandinskys with the Schönbergs.

in 1912, published some of his music and an essay in *Der Blaue Reiter* almanach. The same year, he published his first book, *On the Spiritual in Art*, explaining his own colour theories and his prophecies for the abstract art of the future.

Kandinsky was savagely attacked in the press for his work, although it was now travelling regularly to exhibitions in many different countries. However, the outbreak of war in August 1914 axed further developments and Kandinsky was given 24 hours to get out of Germany. Leaving Gabriele behind, he travelled via Switzerland and the Balkans back home to Russia, arriving on 12 December. He then made a brief trip to Stockholm for an exhibition, and saw Gabriele there for the last time.

Kandinsky remained in Russia until 1921. These were years of poverty and hardship, revolution following on the heels of war. Material goods were hard to come by. From living comfortably on a private income, Kandinsky now found that it could take two weeks to secure a document to buy a pair of shoes, only to discover that there were none available. But such hardships were tempered by Nina de Andreewsky, a beautiful Muscovite years younger than himself, whom he married on 11 February 1917.

AFTER THE REVOLUTION

Kandinsky painted little, producing only 40 pictures from 1914-21 – the amount he had previously completed in a single year. He was kept busy, however, with official functions reorganizing the artistic life of the new Communist state. In 1918, he became a member of the Visual Arts Section in the People's Commissariat for Enlightenment. He helped to set up 22 museums in the provinces and to inaugurate the Institute of Artistic Culture in 1919 and the Russian Academy of Artistic Sciences in 1921. However, his ideals of

The Moscow Years

In October 1917, the Bolshevik Revolution broke out and the Government at the Winter Palace collapsed. During this fraught period, Kandinsky painted very little, producing only a handful of nostalgic views from the window of his apartment overlooking the Kremlin. When the People's Commissariat for Enlightenment was set up, however, he became a member of the Visual Arts Section, and enthusiastically helped to set up 22 new museums in the provinces and organize artistic activities in Moscow. He held many other official posts, but as the Government began to demand cheap art for the proletariat Kandinsky realized that he was out of sympathy with their ideals, and returned to Germany in 1921.

him a job at the Bauhaus, Walter Gropius's model school set up at Weimar in 1919 to promote the uniting of crafts and functional design.

Kandinsky was immediately stimulated by the progressive outlook of the school, where he taught both the life class and mural painting, and once again he started to paint prolifically. At times his work became very close to that of Klee. The two friends enjoyed analysing each other's progress and discussing artistic theories together. Kandinsky set out his principles of geometric construction in his book, *Point and Line to Plane*, published in 1926.

Kandinsky received only a small salary for his work, but an admirer founded a 'Kandinsky Society' for collectors who donated money to the artist in exchange for a watercolour. Evidently there was sufficient income to enjoy summer holidays in Austria, Switzerland, France, Belgium and Italy with Nina.

The Bauhaus days were numbered, however. The organization was regarded as a den of anarchy and Bolshevism by politicians who later joined Hitler's National Socialist Party. Kandinsky and his wife, being Russian, were doubly suspect, and were unjustly denounced in a newspaper as being dangerous agitators. The Bauhaus was forced to move from Weimar to Dessau in 1925, but the Nazi hounding continued, and in 1933 the group was forced to close altogether.

LAST YEARS IN FRANCE

Because of the very tense political climate, Kandinsky moved to France where he spent the rest of his life. He found an apartment in the Boulevard de la Seine, Neuilly, with an attractive view of the Bois de Boulogne. Here he entertained a few chosen friends – mostly foreign artists working in Paris such as Jean Arp and Piet Mondrian. When Kandinsky invited Mondrian to Neuilly to admire the spectacular view from his balcony, the painter of rectangles simply commented, 'Trees! How ghastly!'

Kandinsky became increasingly reclusive, although he was now painting with even more exuberance. By this time, he was using an invented set of symbols, resembling amoeba-like forms as in *Sky Blue* (pp.34-5). When war broke out in 1939 and materials were difficult to come by, he gave up the large canvases and worked on pieces of wood and cardboard. Throughout a prolonged illness in 1944 he was continually planning fresh ventures and new paintings. But he never recovered. On 13 December of the same year, he died of sclerosis.

The artist's apartment
(below) After the rise of the Nazis forced the Bauhaus to close in 1933, Kandinsky left Germany for good. He moved to Paris and this photograph shows the apartment overlooking the Seine where he lived until his death in 1944. The move coincided with a striking change in the direction of his work and the eleven years he spent here are generally regarded as his most controversial.

Bildarchiv Preussischer Kulturbesitz

The artist and friends
(above) Kandinsky – third from right – lived in Moscow for seven years, and although he was kept busy, his output of paintings was low. Initially, he was deeply involved in organizing the artistic life of newly-Communist Russia, but he later became disillusioned when the Government clamped down on the avant-garde.

View of the Kremlin
(left) Kandinsky had a view of the Kremlin from his apartment window in Moscow and the outlook inspired him to do several representational paintings.

Jean-Luc Bohin/Explorer

Abstract Art

Kandinsky was the first artist consciously to reject the image in his art. He spent his life working out a different means of expression in painting.

Kandinksy was the first abstract artist of this century. It is difficult now to imagine what an enormous and courageous leap into the unknown he was taking when he decided to upset the conventions of painting and to turn away from representing the natural world around him. What did he propose to put in its place? Kandinsky spent his whole life working out the answer to this question, and trying to explain his theories in a sequence of articles and books. Both his paintings and his ideas have profoundly influenced the art of this century and continue to do so.

For Kandinsky, art was essentially a spiritual experience. The artist was like a saviour who held the key to the escape from everyday reality. He wanted art to be like music, which appealed directly to the senses and had no need to tell a story, and he believed that colour could be used in the same way as sound. Artists, he thought, should express their emotions through form and colour which would affect the observer's senses, so arousing similar emotions in him or her. The objects, narratives and messages of conventional

Motley Life (1907)
(above) This is an important early work as it contains all the symbols that are important to Kandinsky. Among them are the rider; pilgrim and priest; a boy chasing a girl representing Love, with Death nearby. To construct a picture with so many figures, Kandinsky used a bird's eye perspective.

Study for Composition VII
(right) Once thought to be Kandinsky's first abstract watercolour, this is now thought to be a study for Composition VII.

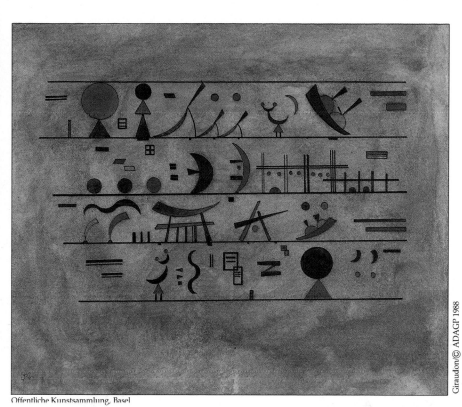

Giraudon/© ADAGP 1988

Offentliche Kunstsammlung, Basel

Rows of Signs (1931)
(above) This resembles a musical score, with the five lines of a stave hung with notes.

Red Oval (1920)
(left) Kandinsky's abstracts of this period had abandoned their free floating forms and become serene rather than apocalyptic.

Photo: David Heald/© ADAGP 1988

Solomon R. Guggenheim Museum

Private Collection. Giraudon/© ADAGP 1988

paintings were only distractions, interfering with an immediate spiritual response to the work of art by focusing on subject matter.

Kandinsky was 30 when he decided to take up painting as a career. He had been stunned by the expressive power of colour in Monet's *Haystacks* at an exhibition of the French Impressionists in Moscow. But it was well over a decade before he produced an 'abstract' painting. His early works were figurative, depicting the magical worlds of Russian folklore and fairytales, as well as the legends of the saints and the iconography of the Orthodox church.

LEARNING FROM OTHER ARTISTS

In Munich and also on his European travels, Kandinsky carefully studied the work of other avant-garde artists. Although they had very little effect on his subject matter, he learnt a great deal about technique from the Art Nouveau artists and the Fauves (Matisse and his followers). Kandinsky adopted the sinuous, decorative line and the

flattened, simplified forms of Art Nouveau in his colour woodcuts. From Matisse and from the old-fashioned glass paintings which he discovered in Murnau, he learnt to compose in broad areas of colour, using a brilliant, luminous palette.

His discoveries about the expressive potential of line and colour were confirmed on the night that he arrived back in his studio and was overwhelmed by one of his own paintings which he did not recognize as it was standing on its side. From this moment, he determined to find a language for his paintings which did not depend on the representation of reality. From 1910 to 1914 he reworked his old motifs, constantly simplifying and abstracting them, so that the eye only very gradually recognized that the abstract shapes in his compositions were actually the old citadels, lovers, mountains, riders and horses reappearing, as in *Improvisation Ravine* (p.27).

Many of these old motifs were apocalyptic symbols for him; for instance, the crumbling citadel and towers and the darkening sun signified impending catastrophe, when the material world would conquer that of the spirit. He often worked from his own glass paintings, where these motifs figured. Then, through a series of sketches, sometimes in watercolour, the forms would become increasingly abstract, until in the final large-scale composition, the original subjects were no longer recognizable.

Kandinsky divided his works into *Impressions*, *Improvisations* and *Compositions*. The *Impressions* (pp.14-15) were quick sketches inspired by 'external nature', the *Improvisations* (pp.24-5, 27) were the spontaneous expressions of his own 'internal nature', and the *Compositions* (pp.28-9) were the much more important, deliberate and fully

19

worked-out paintings which had developed over a long period of time, 'the result of a long and painstaking process of formulating an expression of inner feeling.'

THEORIES ABOUT COLOUR

In 1912, when Kandinsky first published his book *On the Spiritual in Art*, he was not absolutely sure about the ability of non-objective paintings to communicate the artist's intentions, but by the year 1914 he no longer had any doubts. In *On the Spiritual in Art*, Kandinsky outlined his theories on colour. 'Colour', he wrote, 'is the keyboard, the eyes are the hammers, the soul is the piano with many strings. The artist is the hand which plays, touching one key or another, to cause vibrations in the soul'. Every colour had its own characteristics, both physical and spiritual. Colours could recede or advance, grow or diminish in size, they were soft or hard, smooth or rough, and heavenly and profound (like blue) or earthly (like yellow).

In the 1920s, Kandinsky made another breakthrough with the geometrical compositions he painted at the Bauhaus. Using the simple geometrical elements – the point, the line, the circle, the square, the triangle – he analysed the innumerable ways in which these elements could be combined, how they reacted on each other and the effects they produced. He explained the origin of form, how a point is the smallest basic form which creates line when it is moved, and how a line when under pressure becomes a curve. He also showed relationships between shape and colour, like blue corresponding to the circle. In 1926, he published his observations and theories in *Point and Line to Plane*. Later, his work became very varied in composition, using odd motifs and signs, some of which look like microscopic organisms, while others were purely personal hieroglyphs.

With his paintings, Kandinsky was able to take the observer into a completely different world of sensation and emotion, and this new language was his great gift to the 20th century.

Colour and Light

Many artists before Kandinsky used colour and light as expressive elements in their own right, rather than just a means of depicting form. The Impressionist Monet, for example, had a scientific interest in colour and light. When painting, he tried to forget about the objects in front of him, and to see only in streaks and patches of colour, watching how these changed with the varying conditions of light and atmosphere around them. In his late series of waterlilies, he even used colour to create a poetic mood.

Turner, like Monet, composed with colour rather than contrasts of tone, and also used colour in an abstract way to express a mood. He even used it symbolically, as did Kandinsky himself, painting many dramatic scenes of destruction and salvation with fiery skies. Turner had read and been influenced by Goethe's book *Farbenlehre* ('Theory of Colour', 1805-10), which suggests that different colours had different emotional associations.

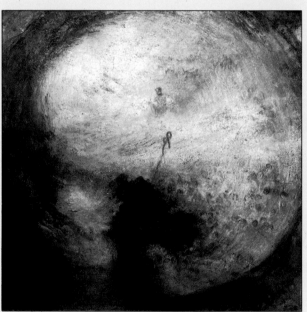

Tate Gallery

© DACS 1988

Art Institute of Chicago

Claude Monet
(1840-1926)
Haystacks
(left) This was a series of 15 paintings in which Monet explored the effect of changing sunlight on haystacks. Kandinsky saw one of them exhibited in Moscow in 1895 and was overcome by the brilliance of colour. He wrote later, 'Painting acquired a fairytale power and . . . the object was discredited as an indispensable element of a painting.'

J. M. W. Turner
(1775-1851)
Light and Colour: the
Morning after the
Deluge
(above) In his later works, Turner's subjects became dissolved in space and light. In this painting, he deliberately employed Goethe's theory of colour, using reds, yellows and greens which the poet associated with warmth and happiness, showing the sun bursting through after the storm.

Composition IV (Battle)

Kandinsky painted *Composition IV* in 1911, just as he was beginning to paint in an abstract manner. At first glance, the picture seems to be an arbitrary arrangement of colour patches and thick black lines, but gradually certain pictorial elements become clear: the blue mountain in the centre with a castle on its crest, three figures in front with red hats holding two spears, the rows of spears on the left indicating a moving army and above them two rearing horses with riders. The soft colours and a reclining couple on the right contrast with the warlike elements and menacing black lines on the left. Kandinsky often painted contrasting themes such as war and peace, intending the emotional overtones to be sensed through colour and form.

TRADEMARKS

Geometric Figures

When Kandinsky rejected the image, he had to find a new means of expression. He turned to the basic geometric forms of circle, triangle and square and explored ways in which they interact to evoke a response in the viewer.

Kunstsammlung Nordrhein-Westfalen, Düsseldorf

© ADAGP 1988

Abstracting the image
(left and detail above)
Composition IV is an excellent example of Kandinsky's process of abstraction. The subjects of the painting have been reduced to forms which make them just recognizable, such as the figures in the centre of the picture, which have been reduced to white patches for clothes and red dabs for hats. The detail of 'horses in a knot' above a rainbow of conciliation, was the subject of a separate painting called Cossacks *(Tate Gallery, London). Kandinsky believed that form without content was 'not a hand, but an empty glove'.*

© ADAGP 1988

Gallery

From his early childhood days in Moscow, Kandinsky reacted with unusual sensitivity to colour. Train at Murnau depicts a scene outside the small house which he shared with Gabriele Münter in the picturesque Bavarian village before the war, but already his intense colours are unnaturalistic. Nature and art were two separate worlds for him, and although he sometimes sketched in the open air, his approach to art was really intellectual and emotional. His most important works were those produced in the studio, like Improvisation 19 and Improvisation Ravine, depicting apocalyptic scenes of man's death and salvation. From 1910 to 1914, as his forms became more and more abstract, he increasingly relied on beautiful and vibrant contrasts of colour to convey emotion. After 1921, when Kandinsky was teaching at the Bauhaus, he began to experiment with the varied and often humorous effects which he could achieve using simple geometrical elements – circles, rectangles, triangles and lines – as in Composition VIII and Swinging. In the final phase of his life, spent in Paris, Kandinsky invented a whole new repertoire of forms, strange and amoeba-like microbes floating in bright background colours as in Sky Blue.

Train in Murnau *1909*
14½″ × 19½″ Städtische Galerie, Munich

From 1908 until the outbreak of the war, Kandinsky and Gabriele Münter used to spend their summer months painting in Murnau, where they bought a house in 1909. It was known as Russenvilla – the house of the Russians – because Kandinsky's friends, Alexei von Jawlensky and Marianne von Werefkin, frequently went to stay. The picturesque houses of the village, the parish church and the railway cutting which Kandinsky saw from the window of Russenvilla became his favourite motifs. The glowing colours in this painting were influenced partly by Jawlensky, who had painted with Matisse, and partly by the simple but expressive stained glass paintings of saints which were still made in the traditional way at Murnau. The work is composed with patches of colour, rather than perspective, and there is a magical toy-like quality about the train and telegraph poles and the little girl waving her handkerchief.

Wassily Kandinsky

Improvisation 19 *1911*
38⅛″ × 41¾″ Städtische Galerie, Munich

Improvisation 19 *was painted on 13 March,*
apparently in one day. Kandinsky called his
Improvisations *'unconscious expressions of an inner*
impulse', and they were very important to him during
this period, when he was working towards abstraction.
He often divided his paintings into areas, the left-hand
side relating to worldly existence, and the right-hand
side to spiritual experience. Here he uses a hieratic scale
to separate the jostling crowd and the colourful
architectural shapes on the left from the unworldly
solemn figures on the right, the colours flowing freely
beneath the thick black lines. Blue for Kandinsky was a
'truly celestial colour' creating a 'supernatural depth'.

Black Lines I *1913*
51½″ × 51½″ The Solomon R. Guggenheim Museum, New York

Kandinsky referred to this bright, cheerful picture as one of his earliest totally abstract works that did not rely on motifs drawn from the natural world. Some have likened the beautiful patches of colour to flowers floating on water, and the angular black lines to mountains, but the artist was not intending to represent these things. He wanted the contrast of the bright free-flowing colours and the scratchy lines to stir the viewer's emotions directly. There is no conventional space in the picture; while the colour patches float freely, the red band subtly anchors them to the surface of the canvas.

Improvisation Ravine *1914*
43¼" × 43¼" Städtische Galerie, Munich

The title commemorates a holiday at Devil's Gorge in Bavaria. Just below the centre of the picture, you can see a couple dressed in Bavarian costume standing on a landing pier, overlooking a waterfall, with two little rowing boats with oars like antennae on the left. But it is not a peaceful, natural scene. It is an apocalyptic explosion of colour and form. From the left a white horse and helmeted rider holding scales on the end of a lance charges into the chaos – one of the horsemen of the Apocalypse. The work was painted just before the outbreak of World War I.

Composition VIII 1923
55⅛″ × 78¾″ The Solomon R. Guggenheim
Museum, New York

Kandinsky painted Composition VIII *while he
was teaching at the Bauhaus, and he regarded it
as one of his most important works. At this time
he was formulating his theories on the physical
and emotional qualities of lines and geometrical
shapes, published as* Point and Line to Plane.
*The painting explores the contrast of dynamic
and static elements: moving diagonal lines; flat
chequerboard areas; colour with or without
depth, translucent or opaque; circles which are
'stable and unstable', 'hard and soft' or
shrinking and expanding.*

Swinging 1925
27¾" × 19¾" Tate Gallery, London

Swinging is concerned with the same experiments as Composition
VIII: elements which create a sense of tension, motion, hardness or
warmth. Here the triangles, segments and other forms are arranged to
create a sensation of swinging and shaking, and this painting was one
of a series which explored the combination of the circle and semi-circle
with the triangle. Kandinsky wrote that the spectator had to look
actively at his works, to 'experience the pulsation of the painting.'

Yellow Painting 1938
45⅞" × 35" The Solomon R. Guggenheim Museum, New York

After Kandinsky moved to Paris he began to use very striking colours, like the vibrant yellow background of this picture and the flat geometrical areas of red, blue, yellow, green, orange and violet. The construction resembles the odd, mechanical figures which appeared in his work in the '30s, but also reflects the influence of Mondrian.

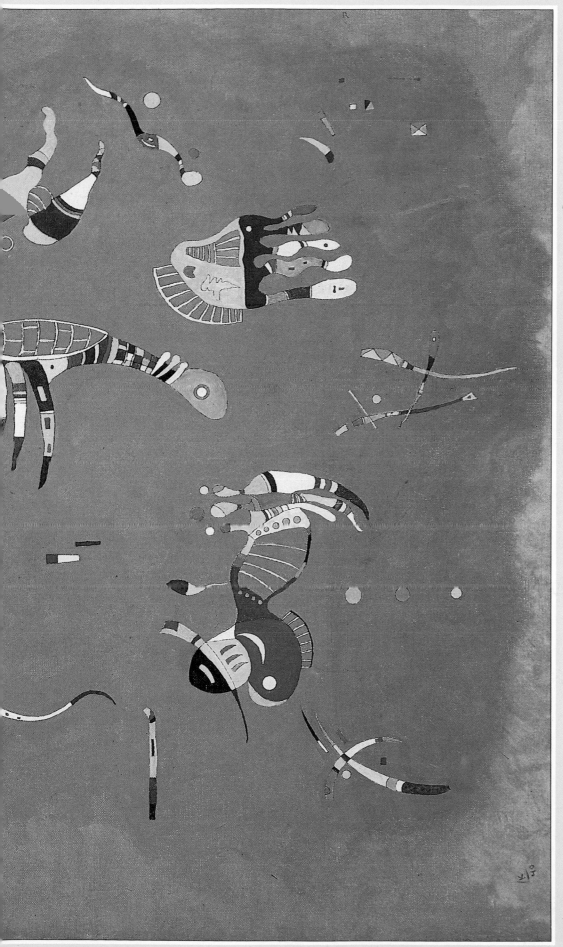

Sky Blue 1940
39⅜" × 28¾" Musée National d'Art Moderne, Paris

The extraordinary creatures in Sky Blue look like tiny microbes floating freely in the air or suspended in water. One of Kandinsky's friends, Fernand Leger, wrote that microscopes were providing a whole new vocabulary of forms for artists, and Kandinsky certainly kept abreast of scientific developments. He wrote that he was amazed by the incredible variety of microscopic fauna on the Normandy beaches, where he sometimes spent the summer months. But the whimsical little creatures come from his imagination as well, and like many of his late works, Sky Blue has a wonderful sense of freedom and invention. Kandinsky was 74 when he painted this work, but it is totally joyful and contains nothing that indicates a fear of impending death.

The Bauhaus

The greatest single influence on design in this century, the Bauhaus attracted some of the most remarkable artists and designers of the day – not least of whom was Kandinsky.

Walter Gropius
(left) The founder of the Bauhaus, Gropius believed that 'the complete building is the final aim of the visual arts'. He set out to unify the hitherto separate art forms of painting, sculpture and architecture through the co-operation of artists and craftsmen.

The Bauhaus stage
(below) A prominent early member of the Bauhaus, Oskar Schlemmer was responsible for sculpture and stage design. His Triadic Ballet – for which this is a sketch – was performed at the 1923 exhibition, and combined his feeling for colour, dance, costume and puppetry.

political unrest, with shortages of food, coal and raw materials devastating the economy. For the first few months, the Bauhaus staff and students were more preoccupied with finding paints and other materials than with studying art and design. There were even disputes about whether wood should be used in the cabinet-makers' workshops or burned in the college stoves.

THE BAUHAUS STAFF

Despite the many hardships and difficulties, Walter Gropius assembled a staff of considerable talent, perhaps the most remarkable of whom was Johannes Itten. Itten was a gifted teacher, but his methods were somewhat bizarre. He was a follower of Mazdazna, a cult whose disciples performed physical and mental exercises, kept to a strict vegetarian diet and fasted regularly. Itten went further by shaving his head and wearing a flowing robe like a monk's habit.

Between 1920 and 1922, Gropius appointed five more teachers at the Bauhaus, including Paul Klee and Wassily Kandinsky who had already established international reputations, and Oskar

'Let us create a new guild of craftsmen without the class distinctions that raise an arrogant barrier between craftsman and artist.' With these words, the Bauhaus – the revolutionary German school of design and the applied arts – declared its radical intentions. No longer were the familiar distinctions between architecture, sculpture and design to remain intact. Instead, the fine and applied arts were taught together under one roof, reinvigorating the traditions of the craftsmen's guilds as well as providing a springboard for the most experimental ideas in modern art.

The creation of the Bauhaus was largely the work of Walter Gropius, who founded the school in 1919 in the ancient German city of Weimar. Before the First World War, Gropius had been one of the country's most promising young architects, designing structures in steel and glass which were startlingly innovative. But his new task was daunting. In 1919, Germany was gripped by

Private Collection

Schlemmer, a painter whose talents encompassed the theatre and ballet. It was Schlemmer's inspiration which created the Triadic Ballet, a form of theatre in which figures in futuristic puppet costume danced against a background of changing dominant colours.

Klee and Kandinsky were responsible for the basic design course at the Bauhaus. Klee was an enthusiastic and conscientious teacher, exploring theories of colour and form in formal lectures and in workshop sessions with the students. Kandinsky on the other hand, had a reputation for dogmatism, and his haughty exterior made many students wary of contradicting him. Even so, one student who was convinced that abstract art was modern nonsense produced a painting for Kandinsky that was entirely white. 'Master Kandinsky,' he quipped, 'I have finally succeeded in painting a picture of absolutely nothing.' Kandinsky was unabashed. Setting the picture on an easel he asked, 'Why did you choose white?' The student replied, 'Because the white plain represents nothingness.' 'God created the world from nothingness,' said Kandinsky, 'so now we must create a little world from nothingness.' With a few brush strokes Kandinsky added a red, a yellow and a blue spot, together with a bright green shadow. The student was dumbstruck. The Master had created a magnificent picture.

A NEW TEACHER

Towards the end of 1922, Johannes Itten left the Bauhaus to be replaced by the Hungarian, Laszlo Moholy-Nagy. Moholy was a self-made artist who could turn his hand to art forms as diverse as photo-montage and typography. His one failing was an inability to speak good German, so that his heavy accent and strange name made him the butt of countless Bauhaus jokes, including a story that he had created a series of paintings by telephoning exact designs to a ceramics manufacturer!

Moholy swept into the Bauhaus like a breath of

The 1923 Exhibition
(above) In 1923, the right wing demanded that Gropius give an account of his work at the Bauhaus. His response was to present an exhibition of products designed and made at the Bauhaus, displayed in an experimental house. Work was also on show in the Bauhaus itself, and in the State Museum, and the event was recorded in a book by Bauhaus members. With contributions by Gropius, Klee and Kandinsky, the exhibition was a resounding success.

The Bauhaus at Dessau
(right) The Bauhaus was in serious jeopardy in 1924 from the new right-wing government of Thuringia – of which Weimar was the capital. The entire Bauhaus community therefore elected to move to the sympathetic climate of Dessau. The city commissioned the new Bauhaus building in 1925, and it was completed within a year. Gropius's design (shown here) has become a landmark of 20th century architecture.

fresh air. His unpretentious manner and passionate belief in modernity helped transform the Bauhaus into a school which taught the elements of technical design, rather than medieval craftsmanship. Indeed, Gropius spelled out this new theme at the Bauhaus exhibition of 1923, when he lectured on 'Art and Technology, a new unity'. The 1923 exhibition was a great triumph, which was fortunate in view of the suspicion and hostility which the school faced from many quarters, from politicians to art critics.

RENEWED ATTACKS

Not surprisingly, perhaps, the school's increasing success caused its enemies to redouble their attacks upon what they called 'the distorted idiots' heads and schizoid scribblings' of its designers. In 1924, right-wing nationalists took power in the Thuringia state parliament, and cut off funds to the

Unifying the arts
(right) The radicalism of the Bauhaus lay in its insistence on unifying the fine and applied arts. The brilliantly coloured weaving, shown here, exemplifies this, in being a 'functional' object as pleasing to the eye as a contemporary abstract painting. Bauhaus students often went on to teach there, as did the designer of this weaving, Gunta Stadler-Stölzl, who played an active part in developing the weaving and textile department of the school.

Peter Keller/Design Council Archives

The importance of crafts
(left) A thorough training in crafts was an antidote to amateurism and academicism. Even a simple object like a cradle had to take account of everyday needs.

Original designs
(below left) The initial experimental course aimed to develop each student's talents without reference to the past. This led to highly original and influential designs, like this bronze teapot.

Marianne Brandt/Design Council Archives

Bauhaus. Only the intervention of the socialist council in the city of Dessau saved the school, and on 4 December 1926, a magnificent new building was opened in Dessau to house the Bauhaus.

The years at Dessau represent the golden age of the Bauhaus. New Masters such as Marcel Breuer, whose revolutionary tubular steel chairs were designed at the Bauhaus, and Gunta Stölzl, a weaver of remarkable talent, developed the ethos of designing for modern living. The appointment of Hannes Meyer to the new post of professor of architecture set the seal upon this approach. Meyer was a socialist who believed that architecture should serve the needs of society by improving the lot of the common man. Together with Gropius, he designed the experimental housing-project in the Toerten district of Dessau. The Toerten estate was one of the first schemes to use standard pre-fabricated components, which were assembled on site.

In January 1928, Gropius decided to resign as director, a move which baffled many of his friends.

The work of Mies van der Rohe
(below) The last director of the Bauhaus, from 1930 to 1933, Ludwig Mies van der Rohe moved the school to Berlin and concentrated activity on architecture, reorganizing the departments. But despite his apolitical stance, the Bauhaus fell victim to Nazism, and in 1938 Mies moved to Chicago. His designs for tall steel and glass buildings – like the Seagram Building in New York (shown here) – are the blueprint of modern architecture.

unrest by closing the Bauhaus for several weeks and dismissing the protesters. The first organized Nazis appeared among the students who replaced them. From then on events moved swiftly.

In 1931, the Nazis gained power in the Dessau city council, attacking the Bauhaus as 'UnGerman, cosmopolitan and Jewish'. In September 1932, the city council voted to shut it down, and on the same day, mobs of Nazis rampaged through the building, breaking up furniture and destroying tools and fixtures.

Mies tried to transfer the Bauhaus to Berlin. But the end came on 11 April 1933 as Hitler and the Nazis consolidated their power across Germany by violently suppressing all forms of political and cultural opposition to their rule. Historically, the Bauhaus was the offspring of the Weimar Republic, with which it shares its lifespan, but its influence has reached beyond that historic epoch to shape our present-day environment.

However, he maintained that 'everything is arranged so that the change of personnel can be taken by the institute without upset'. Gropius suggested that Hannes Meyer should replace him. Meyer emphasized even more the accent upon architecture and design. Students were given important practical tasks to complete before beginning the process of design. One student remembers the importance of having 'to design for present needs'. Before making a cupboard, 'I had to find out the needs of people earning 150-250 marks a month . . . we had to investigate the social conditions of real people'.

FINANCIAL SUCCESS

Under Meyer, many of the workshops became self-financing. The mural department turned out highly successful wallpaper designs and the school won contracts for newspaper and poster advertising campaigns. But, unfortunately, Meyer's political beliefs made him many enemies, and in 1930 he was forced to resign, ostensibly because he had given money to striking miners. It was a move in which Kandinsky had concurred, and the fact that Meyer had doubled the school's income within two years was ignored. In August, Meyer was replaced by Mies van der Rohe and the final act of the Bauhaus had begun.

Mies faced considerable hostility from the Bauhaus students, who believed that Meyer had been stabbed in the back. Mies reacted to student

A Year in the Life 1922

Kandinsky joined the Bauhaus at Weimar when Germany was still being penalized for losing the First World War. Mussolini took power in Italy, Lloyd George lost it in Britain, civil war continued to rage in Ireland and the Greeks suffered a disastrous defeat in Turkey.

The European antagonisms generated by the 1914-18 War had not disappeared by 1922. France, in particular, was bent on making defeated Germany pay as much as possible in the way of reparations for her 'war guilt', despite evidence that these and other war debts were severely damaging the world economy. This vengeful attitude even extended to East European politics: Poland and Germany were in dispute over the rich province of Upper Silesia, but the French commander in charge did nothing to prevent a Polish take-over, despite the fact that a majority had voted for Germany in a referendum. Germany was eventually given most of the province, but its rich mining and industrial areas went to Poland.

Another consequence of France's punitive policy was the Treaty of Rapallo between Germany and Soviet Russia, who

Gandhi behind bars
(above) In March 1922, Mahatma Gandhi (1869-1948) was sentenced to the first of five prison terms. On this occasion, Gandhi, who had begun his doctrine of passive resistance to British rule years before, led a campaign against the payment of taxes to the government, which in one area had flared into violence.

Mustafa Kemel
(right) In 1919, the celebrated Turkish army commander had determined to realize his dreams of a Turkish republic. Travelling through Anatolia, he roused the populace against the allied armies of occupation, setting up an assembly in Ankara which, within a year, formed the basis of a new Turkish state. In 1922 the Greeks agreed on an armistice.

Jean-Loup Charmet

found common ground in being the two 'outcasts' of Europe. Elsewhere anti-Bolshevik hysteria remained strong. In Italy, fear of the 'red menace' worked in favour of the recently founded Fascist party led by Benito Mussolini. Industrial unrest did exist, but the extreme violence of the para-military Fascist squads was responsible for much of the disorder that Fascism promised to cure. The government reacted feebly when Fascists forcibly took control of Bologna and Milan, and on 28 October the Fascists' famous 'March on Rome' took place. This was a demonstration rather than a military action – Mussolini himself went by train – but Fascists were allowed to occupy the city and Mussolini was appointed prime minister. Soon afterwards he was granted temporary dictatorial powers to restore order, and began to remodel Italian society on Fascist lines.

Lloyd George was the only World War I leader who had managed to hold on to power in the new decade. However, in 1921 his popularity was undermined by his over-involvement in foreign affairs at the expense of dealing with Britain's post-war economic depression. In 1922, the Conservatives broke off their coalition with Lloyd George's National Liberals, forcing Lloyd George's resignation as prime minister. He was replaced by Canadian-born Conservative Andrew Bonar Law.

However, Lloyd George did appear to have solved the Irish question, albeit after much bloodshed. It was agreed that Ireland should become virtually independent, with Dominion status, but that Protestant Ulster might opt out. This settlement was rejected by republican intransigents who fought a brief but bitter civil war against the Irish provisional government led by

Civil war
(left) On 6 December 1921, a deputation of Irish moderates signed a treaty with Britain which created an Irish Free State with dominion status, giving Ulster the choice to remain separate. A radical split between those for and those against the treaty escalated into civil war. Here pro-treaty troops of the provisional government fire on a crowd of women protestors outside Mountjoy prison in Dublin.

Fall of Lloyd George
(below) Lloyd George, who had led his country to victory in the Great War, was at the height of his popularity in 1918. Four years later he was out of office, having devoted too much time to foreign affairs at the expense of problems at home.

The 'March on Rome'
(above) The Fascist coup d'état was planned and executed by Mussolini and a quadrumvirate of the three Fascist squad leaders and the secretary of the party. In effect the 'March' was a ramshackle affair which could easily have been repudiated if Victor Emmanuel III had not inexplicably refused to sign an emergency decree.

41

Michael Collins. Meanwhile elections were held by the Irish Assembly (*Dàil Eireann*) to put the issue to the vote. With a majority in favour of the Treaty, an Irish Free State – minus Ulster – was proclaimed in December.

THE BIRTH OF MODERN TURKEY

The year 1922 was disastrous for the Greeks. In the post-war division of spoils, the Turkish possessions of Smyrna, Adrianople and Thrace were ceded to her old enemy Greece, while the outer provinces became allied mandates. However, rebel Turkish nationalists under Mustafa Kemal (Atatürk) defied both the allies and the Ottoman regime. Repelling the Greek advance into mid-Anatolia, they recaptured Smyrna in

1922. The British then withdrew from Constantinople and Kemal entered the city and abolished the old Sultanate in November, declaring Turkey a republic 11 months later.

This was the year when the BBC began regular wireless broadcasts. It was also when the first insulin injections were administered. The Indian Congress leader Mahatma Gandhi was sentenced to six years in prison for anti-British activities. T. S. Eliot published his celebrated poem *The Waste Land* and James Joyce the epic novel *Ulysses*. The novelist Marcel Proust, the explorer Shackleton, and Alexander Graham Bell, pioneer of the telephone, died. And in Egypt, the archaeologist Howard Carter made the find of the century when he and his patron, Lord Carnarvon, entered the tomb of the Pharaoh Tutankhamun and found its treasures still intact.

Robert Harding Picture Library

Popperfoto

Royal treasures
(above and right) Howard Carter's discovery of the tomb of the boy king Tutankhamun was the climax of six years of fruitless excavation in the Valley of the Kings at Thebes. His first view into the tomb on 26 November 1922 was astonishing. By the light of a flickering candle he saw 'strange animals, statues, and gold – everywhere the glint of gold'. That night Carter, his patron Lord Carnarvon, Carnarvon's daughter and *a British archaeologist made an illegal entry into the tomb. For hours the party marvelled at the profusion of exquisite objects in the antechamber such as the magnificent throne whose back, illustrated here, depicts the Pharaoh and his wife. They explored the whole tomb, penetrating the treasury, whose entrance was guarded by a sculpture of Anubis, the fearsome jackal god of the dead, seen here in a contemporary photograph.*

42

KASIMIR MALEVICH
1878-1935

Kasimir Malevich was one of the most radical and innovatory artists working in Russia during the Revolutionary period. Always aware of the latest developments in European avant-garde art, he experimented with a wide range of styles including Impressionism, Primitivism and Futurism, before he formulated Suprematism – the system of geometric abstraction with which his name is identified.

Malevich was a tireless promoter of the Revolutionary cause, helping with propaganda and pageants, teaching in the new art schools and designing imaginary towns for the Soviet state. Nor was his influence restricted to Russia, for his pioneering work as a theorist and designer had important repercussions on architecture, typography, and commercial art in Germany and much of the rest of Europe.

The Independent Revolutionary

**A highly original artist, Malevich came from a peasant background
and had little education. The Russian revolution became a great
source of inspiration to him.**

Kasimir Malevich was born in a village near the Russian town of Kiev in 1878, into a humble family of Polish origin. His father was a foreman at a sugar factory and his mother was an uneducated, and very probably illiterate, peasant woman. Malevich's parents were unable to provide a very sophisticated education for their son but he seems to have absorbed an enormous amount of information and a wealth of ideas through his own reading, which later found an outlet in his prolific, but not always comprehensible, writings on art.

Little is known of Malevich's life, although he did have a daughter. Any impression of Malevich's character has to be patiently pieced together from accounts of him left by friends and colleagues, which generally credit him as being a man of great charm and humour. The records of Malevich's appointments and activities during the Revolution also present a picture of an artist who possessed enormous energy and enthusiasm, and

The artist's mother
This pencil drawing of Malevich's mother was made by the artist in 1900. She was a peasant woman, and lived with her son until her death.

Kiev
Founded in 952 and capital of the first Russian state, Kiev – called the 'mother of Russian cities' – is the capital of the Ukraine and a leading cultural centre for all Russia. The 11th-century cathedral dominates the old city.

Key Dates

1878 born near Kiev

1895-6 attends Kiev School of Art

1904 moves to Moscow

1905-10 works at Roerburg's studio

1913 designs costumes and sets for *Victory over the Sun*

1915 shows 39 abstract pictures at The 0.10 Exhibition of Futurist Painting; publishes *From Cubism to Suprematism*

1917 The Russian Revolution; Malevich joins The Federation of Leftist Artists

1919 moves to Vitebsk and teaches at the School of Art

1927 travels to Germany

1935 dies in Leningrad

who was capable of arousing similar feelings in his audiences when he spoke in public.

Malevich was admitted to the Kiev School of Art when he was 17, but he seems to have left and begun working on his own by 1900. By 1905 – the year of the December Revolution – Malevich had moved to Moscow to continue his studies. The fact that he was arrested for distributing illegal revolutionary material indicates that by this date the left-wing sympathies that were to dominate his life had already formed. Besides the excitement of political turmoil, Moscow during these years had a great deal to offer a young painter fresh from the provinces. Far from being an artistic backwater, the city was in touch with the most advanced and revolutionary developments in French art that had taken place during the previous 40 years.

ART AND MOSCOW

To start with, there was the studio of the avant-garde artist Roerburg, where Malevich worked from 1905 to 1910 and where he was introduced to the work of the French Post-Impressionists such as Vuillard, Bonnard and Cézanne. Then there were the private collections of the wealthy patrons Sergei Shchukin and Ivan Morosov, which contained pictures by the Impressionists, Van Gogh, Gauguin, Matisse and Picasso. These collections were open to anyone who was interested in seeing them, and many Russian

Jack of Diamonds
(below) This was a group of avant-garde artists who exhibited together. Among these were Malevich, Alexei Morgunov (centre) and Ivan Kliun. The latter two became professors after the Revolution.

Malevich influences the Futurists
(above right) This costume sketch by Mayakovsky shows the influence of Malevich. It was for one of the Unclean, heroes of Mayakovsky's play Mystery Bouffe.

artists knew them well. Finally, Malevich found a great deal to interest him in the work of fellow Russian artists. In addition to the Russian Impressionists and Post-Impressionists, there was a younger generation of artists producing Symbolist and Art-Nouveau influenced pictures, and, more importantly, a number of artists who were beginning to investigate Russian folk art.

The two artists who were the leaders of this 'Russian primitivist' movement were Mikhail Larionov and Natalia Goncharova, both of whom came to know Malevich through Roerburg's studio. They were painting scenes of Russian peasant life in the years 1909 to 1911 and their brilliantly coloured canvases, influenced by the traditional decoration of Russian woodcuts, toys and icons, were a revelation to the young painter, who quickly took up the theme of peasant life in his own work. By 1912, he was exhibiting his pictures besides those by Larionov and Goncharova in group exhibitions.

At the same time that he was producing the peasant pictures, Malevich was also experimenting with what he called a 'Cubo-Futurist' style, based upon a synthesis of paintings by Picasso and Braque, and Futurist ideas on art and literature. The Futurist loathing of the art of the past and hidebound tradition corresponded with a growing Russian mood of revolutionary fervour and a desire for change. For the Futurists, art in museums was worthless since real beauty was to be found in the accessories of modern urban

life, such as motor cars, factories, railways and machines. The Russian Futurist poet, Mayakovsky, spoke for many members of his generation when he asked, 'Why look to the past with so much of the future before us?' The Futurists set out to shock the public by their outrageous appearance and behaviour; Mayakovsky took to wearing an orange suit with a spoon in his lapel, and his colleague David Burliuk sported face paintings and a multi-coloured coat.

Even if Malevich himself tended to keep a lower profile in public, he shared the poets' disrespect for the past and their desire to find an artistic expression appropriate to the 20th century. He also collaborated with the Futurist poets on a number of projects. In 1913, he was invited to design the costumes and sets to the poet Alexei Kruchenykh's opera entitled *Victory over the Sun*. The opera told the tale of a man who travelled back in time from the 24th century to 1913, and it had as its central theme the victory of the new order over the old, '. . . over romanticism and empty verbosity', a subject that was dear to Malevich's

heart. The opera itself was shortlived, but the project as a whole had important lasting implications for the artist's career. One of the backcloths he created for it was an abstract design of a square bisected by a diagonal dividing it into one black and one white area: Malevich later described this backcloth design as the origin of his Suprematist style.

SUPREMATISM ON SHOW

However, Malevich did not actually show his first Suprematist paintings until 1915, when he sent 35 abstract pictures to the 0.10 Exhibition of Futurist Painting in St Petersburg (now Leningrad). The paintings, which varied from a simple black square on a white canvas to more complex works, were all combinations of brightly coloured geometrical shapes such as squares, circles and rectangles, and they were viewed as an extraordinary radical departure in art. The word *Suprematist* which Malevich applied to the pictures, was derived from the Latin *Supremus* meaning 'the highest or

Photo: David Heald© ADAGP 1988

Solomon R. Guggenheim Museum, New York

Glass (1912)
(left) This painting by Mikhail Larionov is an example of his theory of 'Rayonnism', which stated that objects emitted rays or lines of force which the artist should manipulate to create his own forms. Rayonnist paintings resemble Futurist works in that they break up the subject into rays or lines, or make the subject disappear completely. The movement was short-lived as Larionov went to Paris in 1915, leaving no followers.

Larionov and Goncharova

From 1909 to 1915, Mikhail Larionov and Natalia Goncharova were the leaders of Russian avant-garde art, and during this period their primitivist style was of crucial importance to Malevich's work. They painted brightly coloured scenes of provincial and peasant life with a directness and simplicity derived from Cezanne and Gauguin, but it was their assimilation of the traditional forms of Russian folk art that gave their work its distinctive character. Around 1911, Larionov began to formulate a Russian verson of Futurism, which he called 'Rayonnism'. Both artists left Russia to go to France as designers with Diaghilev's ballet in 1915.

Gardening (1908)
(right) This work by Goncharova shows the influence of Russian peasant art which so inspired Malevich. She created her own primitive style, inspired by peasant embroideries and wood engravings, using bright patterns of flat colour successfully combined with Fauvist and Cubist influences.

absolute ruler.' He chose the name because it implied that his new style, or system of painting, was supreme over all other types of leftist art. Because it was such a revolutionary new art form, Malevich felt the need to explain it to the public in writing. In 1915, he published a book entitled *From Cubism to Suprematism*, and in the same year he founded a magazine called *Supremus* and delivered a series of lectures with provocative titles like 'The downfall of classics and aestheticism' and 'The Academy and dead painting.' Many critics, not unnaturally, saw Suprematism as an attack on art itself, and the black square became a focus of hatred against an art that seemed negative and baffling to most of those who saw it.

Malevich managed to make a living in the pre-Revolutionary years by teaching and designing. He illustrated Futurist verse, became a leading stage designer and even made patterns for cushions, scarves and embroideries which were produced by peasant women. His rather rarefied Suprematist paintings can never have provided him with much of an income, and in 1917 the

Tate Gallery, London
© ADAGP 1988

Malevich and Matyushin

(above) This photograph shows Malevich and his friend Mikhail Matyushin (centre, with double-breasted jacket) with their pupils in their studio at the Petrograd State Free Art Workshops in 1918. After the Revolution, many art schools were opened and most artists became teachers. Matyushin was also a musician and composed the Futurist opera Victory over the Sun *for which Malevich designed costumes and décor.*

Revolutionary Moscow

The Revolution fired artists with tremendous enthusiasm. The slogan 'Art to the streets' was immediately put into practice by the Futurists hanging their paintings out of windows. Rather naively, Malevich even invited textile workers to his Moscow workshop to study Suprematism, expecting them to change into artists overnight.

Revolution brought about the complete collapse of the art market. Fortunately, Malevich, like many of his contemporaries, found a new source of employment during the Revolutionary years in the several committees that sprang up to formulate artistic policy and education, and in designing Revolutionary propaganda. The Revolution created an unparalleled demand for art. Art schools mushroomed and artists redesigned everything from monuments to postage stamps.

Malevich's commitment to political and artistic renewal was absolute. In 1917, he joined the Federation of Leftist artists, and the following year he began a series of articles in the daily paper *Anarchy* denouncing the old artists' associations which had refused to support the Revolution. It was a happy coincidence that Malevich was able to throw himself into organization at this point in his career because his own experiments with Suprematist painting were reaching a dead-end

Spectrum Colour Library

The Suprematist Legacy

Several of Malevich's pupils became prominent Soviet artists, but Malevich founded no recognizable school of Suprematist painting. Nikolai Suetin was really the only one of his followers to take up and use the style in his own way, and he developed Suprematism into a practical system of design that could be applied to architecture, furniture design, book production and ceramics. In 1927, Suetin helped Malevich design a series of satellite towns for Moscow, although these were never translated into reality. But Suetin's most important work was at the Leningrad Factory, where he was chief designer from 1932-52 and where he devised new types of china, decorated with Suprematist shapes, for mass production.

State Russian Museum, Leningrad

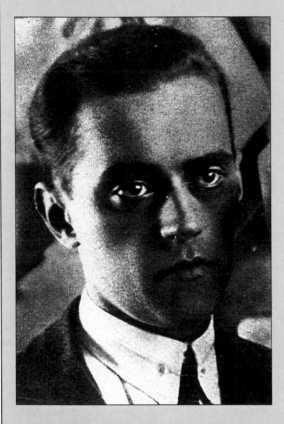

Nikolai Suetin
Suetin developed Suprematism into a style of his own. His perception of space was less grand than Malevich's and his architectural plans were more easily realized. For instance, he helped design the USSR pavilion at the Paris Exhibition of 1937 along Suprematist lines. He was also a designer of furniture, but his most important contribution was to change the look of Soviet ceramics. The simplicity of his design of china (below) was deliberately in keeping with the new aesthetic ideals which reacted strongly against ostentation.

that culminated in the final statement of the 'White on White' series of 1917-18. In 1919, he held a one man show in Moscow entitled *From Impressionism to Suprematism* at which he announced 'the death of Suprematism as a movement in painting': he more or less abandoned easel painting for the next ten years.

The Revolution fostered the notion that easel painting was a form of self-indulgence, and artists were encouraged to leave their studios and take to the streets. 'Artists and writers', wrote Mayakovsky, 'have an immediate duty to get hold of pots and paints and brushes to illuminate, to paint all the sides, foreheads and chests of cities, railway stations and the ever galloping herds of railway carriages.' Malevich and his colleagues began to decorate the streets and squares with abstract shapes and colours derived from Suprematist painting. Elaborate pageants depicting the overthrow of the Romanov dynasty were staged, empty shop windows were filled with posters, and instant monuments to Revolutionary heroes began to appear. One observer said, 'Suprematism has blossomed out in splendid colour all over Moscow.'

THE ARTIST AS ARCHITECT

In 1919, Malevich left Moscow for a two-year period of teaching in Vitebsk, where he took over control of the Art School from Chagall, abruptly informing Chagall that his methods were old-fashioned and irrelevant. Malevich re-named the school 'The College for the New Art', and encouraged his fellow teachers to carry forward the Suprematist style into architectural design, textiles and typography. He now began to produce a series of drawings which he called *Planits*, or 'houses of the future', which look curiously like airborne forms of Suprematism translated into

Tretyakov Gallery-Moscow

The last years of work
(above) At the end of his life, Malevich felt he had exhausted Suprematism and returned to the human form. In Self-Portrait *(left) and* Girl with a Comb, *he combined the traditionalism of artists like Holbein with his own modern style.*

three dimensions. Malevich and his pupils even designed some socialist satellite towns for Moscow, although these dwellings never progressed beyond the planning stage.

The reason that none of the buildings that Malevich drew on paper was ever built is that his architectural designs were highly impractical. Malevich was producing Utopian dreams of futuristic cities rather than blueprints for real towns, and this is where his entire approach differed from that of his Constructivist colleagues like Tatlin and Rodchenko, who were committed to the idea of creating functional objects. Despite his involvement in some of the applied arts, Malevich really believed that art was an essentially individual and spiritual activity. He felt that although practical design could draw upon fine art for inspiration – just as elements of Suprematist painting were used to create propaganda art, ceramics and textiles – it was not the job of the artist to enmesh himself in the mundane problems of design. Something of this belief is reflected in Malevich's teaching methods, which he put into practice at art schools in Vitebsk, Moscow and Leningrad in the 1920s. The artist thought that it was not his business to impose his own rigorous aesthetic system on his pupils, as it was much more important to foster individuality in art and to help each of his pupils discover the unique direction of his or her talent. Malevich felt that each artist had his own individuality to communicate, and his reluctance to shape his pupils into a particular mould may help explain

why he founded no established school of Suprematist art, although some of his pupils – Suetin for example – did take up and develop the style in their own way.

It is also strange that while Malevich had turned away from painting in the decade following the Revolution, he nonetheless staged several exhibitions of his pictures at home and abroad. In 1927, he even accompanied his own one-man show to Germany, where he was able to meet the German avant-garde artists, designers and architects of the Bauhaus who so admired his work and were very much influenced by it.

A NEW APPROACH

Malevich enjoyed his fame as a radical artist, yet within three years of the Berlin exhibition he had returned to figurative painting. Perhaps the reason for this sudden change of artistic approach is linked to Malevich's perception of Suprematism and abstract art as the embodiment of the ideals held during the early 'heroic' years of Communism. He may have felt that the style was inappropriate to the grim realities of life under Stalin during the 1930s, when the vision of a perfect new world that he and his contemporaries had sought to create was rapidly receding.

Yet any dissent that Malevich may have felt in private probably went unvoiced. His reputation with the Soviet art establishment remained intact. When he died in Leningrad in 1935 leaving instructions that his remains were to be transferred to a coffin bearing Suprematist designs, the city council insisted on bearing the cost of the funeral in homage to his services to Russian art.

Last days of life
(below) When Malevich died he was placed in a coffin he himself had designed along Suprematist lines. He lay in state at the Leningrad Artists' Union and a large crowd made up the funeral procession to the station. His ashes lie buried at Nemchinovka, just outside Moscow. His family were granted a pension by Leningrad council.

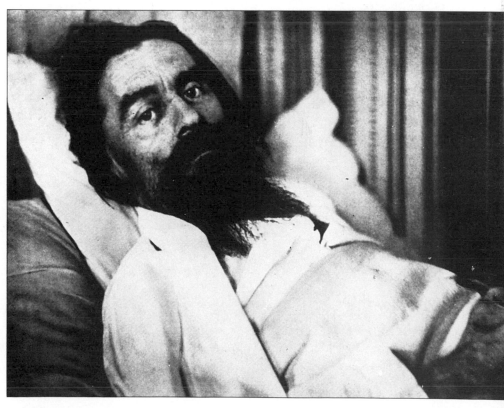

A Radical Vision

A great experimenter at a time of fundamental political and artistic change, Malevich created one of the purest yet most influential abstract art movements of the 20th century – Suprematism.

Malevich was a remarkably eclectic artist. He experimented with a wide variety of styles and influences before he developed the revolutionary Suprematist manner for which he will always be remembered. Although it is often hard to date Malevich's paintings precisely, any general survey of his work reveals that the artist often made sudden transitions from one style to the next, rather than following a pattern of more gradual evolution. It is as though Malevich saw painting as an intellectual exercise, or a scientific experiment whose methods were to be abandoned once a satisfactory conclusion was reached.

The earliest known works by Malevich date from about 1904 and are very much in the Impressionist style, showing the influence of the artist's first contacts with works by French painters in Moscow collections. These early pictures have the feathery brushstrokes and light pastel colours used by the Impressionists, but Malevich never really shared their concern with trying to capture the transient reality of the natural world. For one thing, Malevich painted people as though they were types rather than individuals, and he never sought to render perspective convincingly; even his earliest pictures look two-dimensional.

A Private of the First Division. 1914
(below) Cubism gave Malevich the impetus to examine different forms of representation. Here he uses collage, lettering and abstract areas of colour, together with fragmented details, like the soldier's eye and ear. The effect, if bizarre, has a certain humour.

Stedelijk Museum, Amsterdam

21⅛" × 17⅝" oil on canvas with collage of postage stamp, thermometer, etc.

Collection, The Museum of Modern Art, New York

The Woodcutter (1912)
(left) This is a prime example of Malevich's Cubo-Futurist phase. The figure and background are perceived as cylinders merging to form an image of machine-like tension.

Pamphlet cover (1920)
(right) In the years after the Revolution, Suprematism embraced all art forms. Just one example is Malevich's design for a pamphlet by the art critic, Nikolai Punin.

This tendency towards an unnaturalistic presentation of the world became more extreme when Malevich began to paint scenes of peasant life. In these, monumental figures are set against a backdrop of simple shapes based upon elements in the landscape, rather than a detailed depiction of the countryside itself. Works such as *Woman with Buckets and Child* show the influence of Cézanne and Gauguin in their use of large areas of flat colour bounded by blue or black outlines, but they are given a particularly 'Russian' feel by their association with traditional forms of Russian art. The massive and rather static figures with their elongated faces recall the Madonnas, saints and priests in Russian icons.

THE CUBO-FUTURIST PERIOD

Interest in the work of Cézanne eventually led Malevich to follow the French artist's famous dictum and analyse nature in terms of cylinders, spheres and cones. In pictures dating from Malevich's 'Cubo-Futurist' period, the figures gradually become fused with the landscape, and both are painted using similar shapes so that they look as though they are part of a colourful patchwork. This blending together of man and environment – visible in works such as *The Rye Harvest* (p.56) – conveys a sense of agricultural work as part of the unending rhythm of nature. The addition of a metallic sheen to the paint surface gave a new dimension to this idea, since the shiny cylinders and cones that make up the later peasant pictures resemble the moving parts of a vast machine. In these paintings, Man seems to have lost his individual identity and become part of his work. In *The Knife Grinder* (p.57), painted during Malevich's Cubo-Futurist phase, the process is taken one step further, and the knife grinder's body disintegrates into a moving blur caught up in the frenzied action of the machine.

At the same time that Malevich was producing these disturbing images of men at work, he was also developing a more abstract manner based upon the Cubist collages of Picasso and Braque. Collage, and the paintings that resemble it, gave

Buildings of the future
(below) When Malevich conceived the Suprematist movement, he already had in mind its three-dimensional possibilities. His idea of building was cosmic and Utopian. In 1918 he wrote, 'Let tall needles and flying houses prepare to take off. Let wedge shapes cleave the bosom of space.' Part of the development of Suprematism from 1923 to 1929 involved the creation of architectons – wood or plastic architectural models, like this one. Malevich's designs did not, however, become an immediate reality – and perhaps never will.

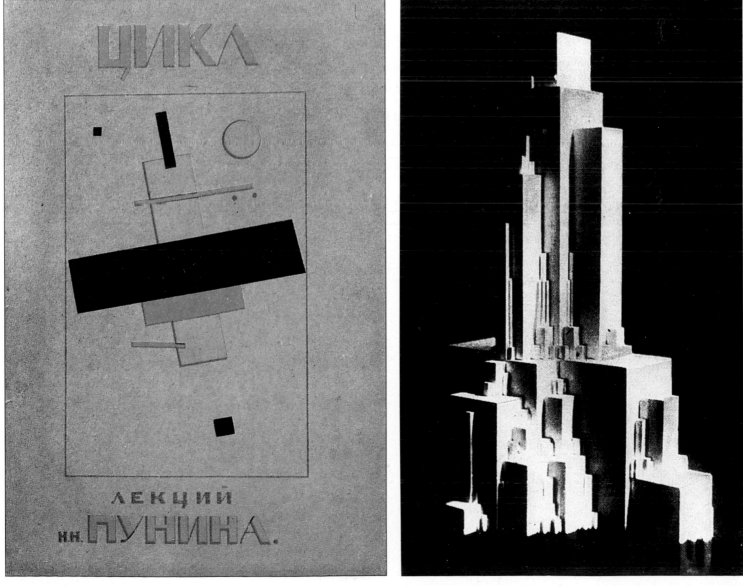

Experiments with Abstraction

In the early years of the 20th century, artists all over Europe were experimenting with abstract art, but not all of them made such an abrupt transition from figurative work to total abstraction as Malevich did. About the time he was painting his first Suprematist canvases, Mondrian in Holland was creating pictures where the grid, which was to become the feature of his abstract work, was starting to emerge. In Germany, Kandinsky was painting a series of *Improvisations* in which certain figurative elements still appear among the more abstract shapes and swirls of colour that prefigure his later work.

National Gallery of Art, Washington/Ailsa Melon Bruce Fund

Gemeente Museum, The Hague

Piet Mondrian (1872-1944) **Flowering Apple Tree** (*left*) *Mondrian's cycle of tree paintings of 1909-12 shows his gradual but clear progression from naturalism to complete abstraction.*

Wassily Kandinsky (1866-1944) **Improvisation 31 (Sea Battle)** (*above*) *Kandinsky's* Improvisations *were crucial in his transition to free form (see also pp. 24-7).*

Malevich an opportunity to throw together lettering, objects, and flat geometrical areas of colour to create a bizarre jumble of images. In *A Private of the First Division* (p.50), fragments of soldier, words and numbers hover in space, giving an effect that is comical and surreal. It is curious to remember that at the time Malevich was creating works like this, he was also painting his first Suprematist paintings, which are fundamentally different in conception. While the collages play upon the meaning of images, Suprematism bans them from the canvas, reducing painting to its most basic elements of form and colour.

THE LOGIC OF SUPREMATISM

Malevich himself described Suprematism as 'a hard cold system set in motion by philosophical thought', and his division of Suprematism into three phases of development – black and white, coloured, and white – reinforces this impression of logical experimentation. The visitor to the 0.10 Exhibition of Futurist Art in 1915 would have seen an apparently rational progression from the simplest shapes of the first Suprematist pictures – a black square on a white canvas, a black circle on a white canvas, and a black cross on a white canvas – to more complex compositions involving rectangular bars of black, red, green and blue.

In the later paintings, dynamic elements were introduced. Diagonal axes and the foreshortening of circles into ellipses and rectangles into rhomboids, created an illusion of a third dimension, and of objects moving in space. Although some of the early Suprematist paintings had rather puzzling titles, such as *Painterly Realism of a Footballer*, which gave them some link with the visible world, these were gradually abandoned, and Malevich's art became entirely non-representational and abstract in its intention. When the artist stated in 1916, 'I have destroyed the ring of the horizon and stepped out into the circle of things', he meant that he had freed himself from the need to describe the outside world, and that he was now free to paint such intangible entities as cosmic space and the sensation of flight.

Suprematism was a revolutionary movement, but its very rigidity ensured that it had a finite lifespan. Malevich's 'white on white' series of 1917-18, in which the merest suggestion of a white square is pencilled in against a white background, marks Suprematism's natural end. However, it remained fundamental in helping to change the way in which artists saw the world, and stands as one of the most radical of the early 20th-century experiments with abstraction.

Suprematist Painting 1916

Malevich painted this picture during his second 'coloured' phase of Suprematism, when his work had progressed from the simple black, white and red shapes of the earlier pictures to more complex assemblies of rectangles, squares and lines. He had also begun to introduce a sense of dynamism into his work, and here the strong diagonal axis conveys an impression of upward movement. The white background gives a feeling of infinite space, while the fact that the shapes are different sizes suggests they are hovering on different planes.

The potential of shape and colour
(left and detail above) In this painting, Malevich plays off movement against stasis. The strong dynamic sense given by the fragmented shapes as they shoot upwards is interrupted by the insistent horizontal of the black bar near the centre of the composition. Malevich also clearly enjoyed playing upon the visual peculiarities of colour. As yellows and reds appear to advance, and darker tones to recede, he creates further cross movement.

Stedelijk Museum, Amsterdam

Gallery

At the beginning of his career Malevich was affected by various foreign influences (mainly French), both traditional and avant-garde. In his 30s he began to forge a distinctive style by combining these foreign influences with Russian themes and motifs, as in The Rye Harvest and The Knife Grinder, both painted in 1912. His

On the Boulevard *c.1903*
21½" × 26½" Writers' House, Leningrad

Malevich's early paintings give no indication of the revolutionary direction his art would take. He started working in a conventional style based on the work of the French Impressionists, whose art was well known and much admired in Moscow at this time. This charming scene shows his delight in observing the varied details of the world around him. Later in his career, when he had turned to abstract art, Malevich was to condemn representational art as 'theft from nature'.

momentous contribution to the development of modern art, however, dates from 1915 when he launched Suprematism. He banished all trace of subject, relying on the subtle interaction of shape and colour to produce his hauntingly beautiful effects. Some of these pictures, such as Suprematist Painting (1915) are quite 'busy' and colourful, but in his White Square on White, he arrived at the extreme point of austere simplicity. Perhaps not surprisingly, it is difficult to be sure which way up Malevich intended his paintings to be seen particularly as in photographs of contemporary exhibitions, the same picture is sometimes shown hanging in different ways.

Portrait of a Member of the Artist's Family *c. 1904*
26¾″ × 39″ Stedelijk Museum, Amsterdam

Little is known of Malevich's family background, and we do not know exactly who the sitter in this portrait is; here he gives little away and seems to be more interested in depicting the effects of sunlight on the varied surfaces than in revealing anything about the woman's personality. At this time, the artist was still heavily influenced by 19th-century French painting and the richly worked paint surface reveals a debt to Post-Impressionism.

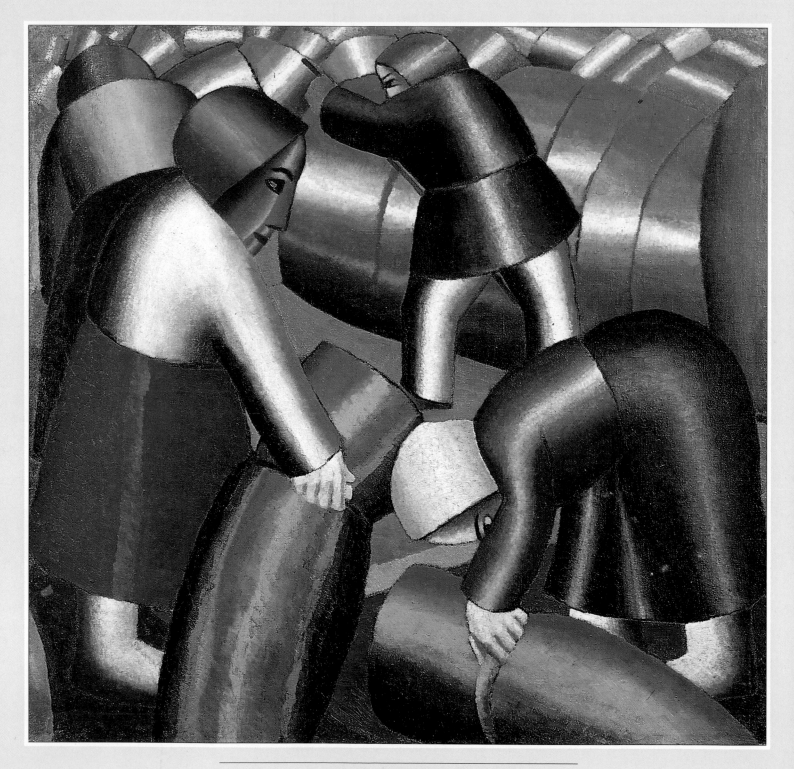

The Rye Harvest *1912*
28¼″ × 29¼″ Stedelijk Museum, Amsterdam

Malevich showed a number of paintings of peasant scenes at the avant-garde 'Donkey's Tail' exhibition in Moscow in 1912, of which this is the best known and most impressive. The massive tubular forms marked a move away from the comparative naturalism of his early work and capture the heaviness of the peasants' labour.

The Knife Grinder *1912*
31¼″ × 31¼″ Yale University Art Gallery

*One of Malevich's most celebrated works, this dynamic painting is
strongly influenced by the contemporary work of the Italian Futurists
in the way in which the forms are fragmented and multiplied. But
whereas the Futurists were intoxicated by the excitement of machines
in motion, Malevich portrays an individual at work.*

oil on canvas

Suprematist Composition: Red Square and Black Square *(1914/15?)* 28″ × 17½″ Collection, The Museum of Modern Art, New York

Malevich first exhibited works of this type, which he called Suprematist art, in 1915. He wrote, 'The Suprematists have deliberately given up the objective representation of their surroundings in order to reach the summit of the true "unmasked" art and from this vantage point to view life through the prism of pure artistic feeling.'

Eight Red Rectangles *1915*
22½″ × 19″ Stedelijk Museum, Amsterdam

Malevich's Suprematist paintings are constructed of basic geometrical shapes – the square, the rectangle, the circle, the cross, the triangle – and a severely restricted range of colour. There is no sense of three-dimensional space in paintings such as this, but they sometimes, as here, convey a feeling of floating or falling.

oil on canvas/Purchase

Suprematist Composition: Airplane Flying *(1914)*
22⅞″ × 19″ Collection, The Museum of Modern Art, New York

---

*Although Malevich constructed his pictures without reference to the
visual world around him, he sometimes gave them titles that suggest
the dynamic nature of the composition. From its earliest days,
machine-powered flight made a great impact on Russian artists and
aviation was seen as a symbol of world progress.*

The Football Match *1915*
27½″ × 17¼″ Stedelijk Museum, Amsterdam

*As with the painting on the opposite page, the title here evokes the
idea of dynamic motion rather than referring to any specific
representational content (however residual) in the painting. Malevich
said that the artist must construct his work 'on the basis of weight,
speed and the direction of movement'.*

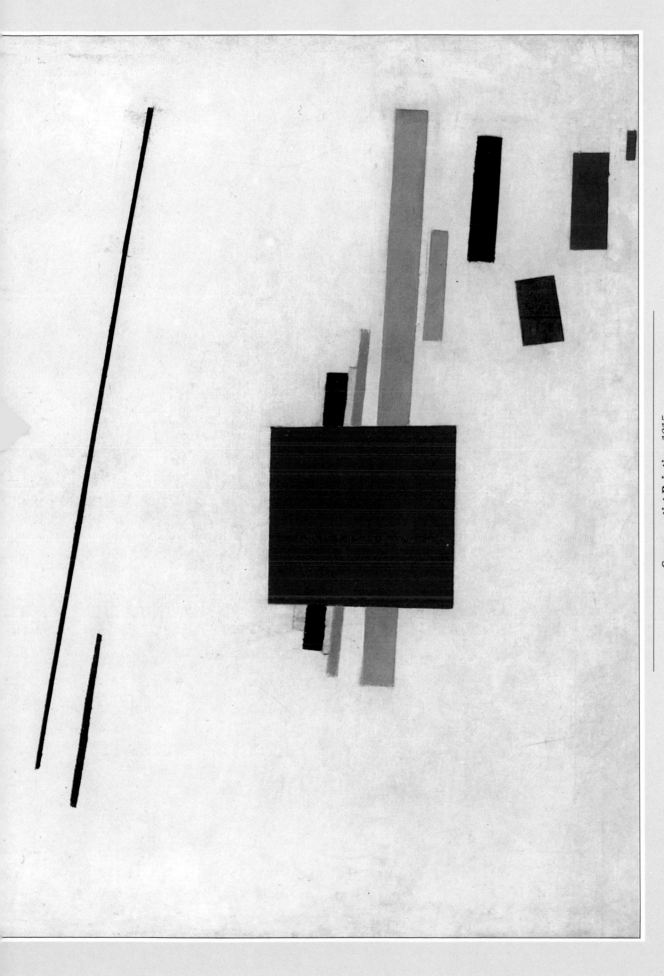

Suprematist Painting 1915
40" × 24½" Stedelijk Museum, Amsterdam

Although Malevich still confines himself here to geometrical shapes and basic colours, he has made the composition more complex than in many of his Suprematist paintings by overlapping the forms. In so doing he creates a hint of spatial depth, and the overall effect is one of incipient movement.

Suprematist Composition *(1916/17?)*
38½" × 26⅛" Collection, The Museum of Modern Art, New York

*In this painting Malevich softens his approach in comparison with the
Suprematist paintings illustrated on the previous six pages. The
ellipse cut in half by the bottom of the picture introduces a more
complex and sensuous shape and the colours are mainly subtle pastel
tints. Malevich was of a metaphysical turn of mind and the effect he
produces here is ethereal and other-worldly, suggesting the mysteries
of the expanding universe.*

Yellow Parallelogram on White *1917-18*
41¼″ × 27¾″ Stedelijk
Museum, Amsterdam

In this startlingly bold picture Malevich both simplifies and complicates his attitude to form – simplifies in that the 'image' is reduced to one shape; complicates in that he abandons geometric principles in the way one edge of the shape gradually fades into the 'background'. The effect produced is extremely dynamic, suggesting a great comet blazing through space.

oil on canvas

Suprematist Composition: White on White *(1918?)*
31¼″ × 31¼″ Collection, The Museum of Modern Art, New York

Malevich regarded the square as the 'purest' of the geometric forms
and here he reached the ultimate distillation of his ideas. After
painting a series of such 'white on white' pictures, he realized he
could travel no further along this road and, in the 1920s, he reverted
to figurative painting.

Russia in Turmoil

Malevich's revolutionary artistic style evolved against a background of increasing dissatisfaction with the Tsarist regime. In 1917, the Bolsheviks seized power, changing the face of Russian society.

By the end of 1916, the Russian Empire was in a desperate plight. Her armies in the West were thoroughly demoralized, and while that was a common enough symptom anywhere in Europe after more than two years of unprecedented slaughter, the Russians were at breaking point. They were led in the field by Tsar Nicholas II, a weak-minded man who showed no more imagination as a general than he did in any other capacity. Shattered armies left behind them starving cities – starving because the demands made on the railway system by the armies hindered the transportation of food from the vast southern prairies to the densely-packed western

The dissolute monk
(right) Cartoons of the time savagely lampooned Rasputin's powerful position at the Russian court. A lascivious charlatan, he ingratiated himself with the Tsarina through his apparent ability to help the young Tsarevich, who suffered from haemophilia: through the Tsarina, Rasputin influenced the Tsar.

Novosti Press Agency

Novosti Press Agency

The plight of the masses
(above) After the emancipation of the serfs in 1861, social reform was slow to come. Peasants and workers – the vast majority of the Russian population – eked out a meagre existence in appalling conditions, and often died of starvation.

A spontaneous uprising
(right) The February Revolution began on 23 February, 1917 as a series of strikes and riots on the streets of Petrograd. These developed into a massive popular demonstration against the rule of the Tsar, forcing abdication.

cities. Those peasants left on the land were hoarding food, hoping to cash in on soaring black market prices. The government, such as it was, was incompetent where it was not corrupt, and the Court bordered on the insane. The Empress Alexandra was herself in thrall to the demonic Rasputin, a self-styled 'holy man' who wielded immense influence in matters of state. Just before the New Year, Rasputin was brutally murdered by a group of his enemies, after which followed a chain of events that finally brought about the collapse of the Tsarist rule.

WIDESPREAD UNREST

Political action was now taking place at regular intervals in the streets, especially the streets of Petrograd (or St Petersburg, now Leningrad). Workers in their thousands staged strikes and demonstrations as a gesture of profound despair with their situation and, even in remote villages, peasants were resisting officialdom of every sort. Discipline was breaking down in the army, and traditional appeals to the soldiers' patriotism fell on deaf ears. Desertions from the Front threatened to become a stampede.

The rudimentary parliament, or Duma, which had been in existence for just over a decade, was a natural focus of demands for reform, but it was powerless to control events. Vladimir Ilyich Ulyanov – better known to the world as Lenin – was still out of the country, having been exiled in

Kasimir Malevich

Тов. Ленин ОЧИЩАЕТ землю от нечисти.

1895 for his revolutionary activities. His remarkable vision and leadership powers were to play a crucial role, but this was not to happen for another eight months. In the meantime, the entire edifice of the Russian state seemed to be crumbling, and nowhere could sufficient resolution be found to prevent that happening. In February 1917, these fears were realized.

While the Tsarist government attempted to dismiss the Duma, soldiers and workers joined forces to organize a rival centre of power, which they called the Petrograd Soviet. On 23 February, there was a vast, spontaneous demonstration in the streets of the capital. The political slogans were blunt: 'Down with Autocracy!', 'Down with War!'. The Petrograd garrison was showing signs of mutiny, and some army commanders admitted that the situation was beyond their control. The stark truth of this was shown two days later when Tsar Nicholas ordered the armed forces to fire on the demonstrators. After refusing to obey, unit after unit began going over to the protesting workers. Total anarchy threatened, and faced with that terrible prospect the Duma finally

Communist beginnings

(above) After Lenin seized power, artists were quick to take up the Bolshevik cause. This poster shows Lenin sweeping the world clean of the kings, generals and bankers who were masters of the old society. In reality the Bolsheviks faced determined opposition from Tsarists and other political factions, and after peace was made with Germany in 1918, the Russians found themselves embroiled in an equally bloody civil war.

Leon Trotsky
*(left) A brilliant orator
and organizer, Trotsky
played a crucial role in the
October Revolution, and
as War Commissar of the
Bolshevik Government,
led the Red Army to
victory in the Civil War.*

Early priorities
*(below) Posters like this
formed part of the new
régime's vigorous
campaign against
illiteracy. Here illiteracy
is likened to blindness
which leads the peasant to
failure and misfortune.*

exiled to Siberia by the Tsarist regime, had spent the first half of the war in Switzerland. In April 1917, the Germans enabled him to slip back into Russia, believing – rightly as it transpired – that throwing such a volatile factor into the confused equation of the new Russia would paralyse that country's capacity to stay in the war. At Finland Station in Petrograd, Lenin received a hero's welcome and in a matter of days, had established himself as the leader of the Marxist organization, the Bolsheviks. A month later, Leon Trotsky, a brilliant and proven agitator, returned to Petrograd from exile in Paris. He quickly joined forces with Lenin, and his genius for revolutionary improvization combined with Lenin's ruthless determination proved irresistible. The Bolsheviks demanded an immediate end to the war, and they employed wrecking tactics to bring the existing administration to a standstill. On 25 October 1917,

showed a firm resolve. On 2 March, it formed a provisional government, with the backing of the Petrograd Soviet. Late that evening the Tsar tamely abdicated, and the old Russian order vanished with him.

The traumatic events of February 1917 were felt right across Europe and beyond, in the United States. The overthrow of the Tsarist regime was widely welcomed by people of liberal persuasion, both for its own sake and because it made the Allied cause in the war more respectable, being now clearly perceived as a war between democracies and non-democracies. This had a particular influence on the debate then raging in the United States, as to whether or not the Allied cause had sufficient moral justification to warrant America's intervention on its side.

There was, however, alarm that the new Russian 'order' would take Russia out of the war, thus throwing the German and Austrian armies into the stalemated war in the West. As this was now literally draining the lifeblood of an entire generation of British and French men, the thought was horrible to contemplate. Immense pressure was thus brought to bear on the new government, increasingly under the sway of the socialist Alexander Kerensky, to continue with the war. It was the attempt by this government to do so – coupled with the return of Lenin – that was to cause its downfall.

Lenin had been a long-standing revolutionary socialist, and after being variously imprisoned and

НЕГРАМОТНЫЙ тот-же СЛЕПОЙ
ВСЮДУ ЕГО ЖДУТ НЕУДАЧИ И НЕСЧАСТЬЯ·

a relatively bloodless coup – the only notable drama being the storming of the Winter Palace – brought the Bolsheviks to supreme power.

The Bolsheviks had promised a complete break with the past, but as Lenin knew with his characteristic certainty, immediate peace was the prerequisite for national survival, and for the untried Communist experiment. It turned out to be peace at any price. The Treaty of Brest-Litovsk, signed with Germany in March 1918, was a humiliation, involving the loss of huge amounts of territory in the west. However, it did provide some kind of breathing space.

The Bolsheviks had seized power in confusing circumstances, and they did not command support from the majority of their fellow citizens. In order to consolidate their position, they abolished the Duma and then proceeded to wage a propaganda campaign against the entire capitalist

May Day
(right) The celebration of May day had been forbidden under the Tsar. After the Revolution it took on a new ideological significance and became one of the main holidays of the year.

Spreading the word
(below) The Bolsheviks used every possible form of propaganda to gain support for the Revolution: special trains and boats went across the country filled with speakers and brass bands.

world. The motive was partly ideological, for a central tenet of Communism was that it was an international creed. However, there were also pragmatic reasons, since Lenin and Trotsky believed that once the war ended, the 'winning side' would be implacably hostile to the new Soviet state and would not hesitate to attack it.

This was no paranoid delusion. Allied and American soliders soon found themselves fighting on Russian soil, initially in an attempt to keep open the Eastern Front. After the war with Germany finally ended in November 1918, however, their role became more sinister. The Bolsheviks had a host of enemies at home – ranging from hardened Tsarists to democratic Socialists who deplored Lenin's blatant contempt for democracy – and a number of civil wars broke out. The victorious Western powers, throughly alarmed at Bolshevik propaganda inciting their own working classes to rise up in violent revolution, took the side of the various anti-Bolshevik factions. It was not until November 1920 that this last sorry stage in the lengthy conflict dragged to an end, and the Soviet Union was left in peace, and to the Herculean task of resurrecting a prostrate nation according to its revolutionary ideology. This somewhat half-hearted attempt by the Western countries to squash the new Soviet state left permanent scars and hardened attitudes on both sides, to such an extent that the mistrust between Soviet Union and the Western democracies is still the dominant factor in global affairs.

Malevich's abstract *Black Square* of 1915 acquired a symbolic appropriateness as World War I settled into blood-soaked futility. During this momentous year, the Allies met with disaster in the Dardanelles, the *Lusitania* was sunk, Italy entered the war, and poison gas was used for the first time.

The grim realities of 'the Great War' became apparent as 1915 came and went with much bloodshed and little change in the West. Both sides launched offensives – the Allies in Neuve Chapelle, Aubers and Loos, the Germans at Ypres – which made slow and terribly costly progress in the face of barbed wire and machine guns. The Germans gained some advantage with poison gas, but the Allies quickly followed suit.

In Eastern Europe the armies were more mobile, but the war also ran to a pattern: the Russians generally defeated the Austrians, but were outmatched by the Germans, who after two mighty offensives entered Warsaw and conquered all of Poland. Russia's desperate needs for supplies encouraged her allies to try to break through the Straits leading into the Black Sea, which were controlled by hostile Turkey. But the

Norman Wilkinson/Troops landing on 'C' Beach, Suvla Bay/Trustees of the Imperial War Museum, London

Landing at Suvla Bay
(*above*) *In January 1915, the British War Office agreed to mount an expedition to take the Gallipoli peninsula with Constantinople as its object. Landings by British, Australian and New Zealand troops were made on 25 April, but fierce Turkish resistance kept them pinned down on the coast with many losses. Further landings at Suvla Bay in August failed despite the courage of the troops. Trench warfare resulted and evacuation was soon recommended.*

'Papa' Joffre
(*right*) *The optimism of the French commander-in-chief although misplaced, endeared him to his troops and gave him virtual control of the allied army on the Western Front (1914-16).*

GENERAL JOFFRE

The horrors of war
(*above*) *Gassed and Wounded by British war artist Eric Kennington is a mute reminder of the horrors of trench warfare. On 22 April, 1915, the German army first launched a new and terrible weapon on the Ypres salient – poison gas. However, its inventors had failed to realize that not only would they need protection against their own gas as they advanced, but a possible change in wind direction could make it a double-edged weapon. The gas mask quickly became an essential article of military equipment on both sides.*

Jean-Loup Charmet

consequent Dardanelles campaign turned into a disaster. British warships failed to force their way through the Straits, and in April and August, British, Australian and French troops landed on the Gallipoli peninsula, only to be pinned down on the beaches by the Turkish defenders; in December, after very heavy loss of life, the humiliated Allies withdrew.

THE EXPANDING CONFLICT

The British were rather more successful against the Turks in the Middle East, throwing them back from the Suez Canal and also advancing victoriously into Mesopotamia. But in November, the British force was checked at Ctesiphon and fell back to Kut-el-Amara, where they were besieged.

Russia's difficulties and the Dardanelles fiasco had decided Bulgaria to throw in her lot with the Central Powers. In September, a joint Austro-German and Bulgarian offensive overran Serbia, despite the intervention of Anglo-French forces which landed at Salonika on the Greek mainland. The Greeks remained neutral, though the political situation in the country was very unstable, but it was perfectly clear that the Allies intended to make use of their territory whether or not the Greeks were agreeable. In the meantime, the Serbs began their epic march through the mountains to Albania, and arrived at Scutari in November.

Many Italians were gripped by war fever, including the editor of the socialist paper *Avanti*, Benito Mussolini, who broke with his party on the issue and so began his career as an ardent

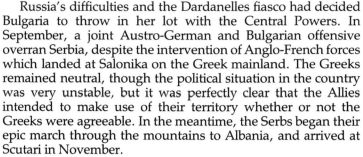

Russian futurist
(right) For Vladimir Mayakovsky (1893-1930), the Russian poet, artist and playwright, 1915 was an important year. He participated in the art exhibition '1915' along with such luminaries as Larionov, Goncharova, Chagall, Kandinsky and Tatlin; he completed one of his most celebrated poems, A Cloud in Trousers, *and perhaps most important, he met the couple Osip and Lili Brik. Osip published Mayakovsky's poem in September and Lili became the mistress and great love of Mayakovsky's life.*

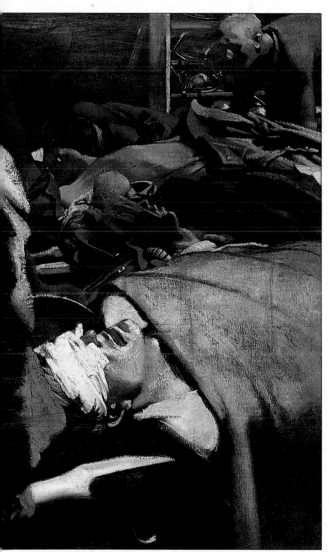

The spreading war
(right) While German and Allied troops were locked into what would prove to be another three years of trench warfare and the war in the east continued to be fought on shifting fronts, the conflict which had sucked in Turkey and colonial territories all over the world continued to expand in 1915. Turkey sent an army across the Sinai Desert to cut off the Suez canal; Italy entered the war on the side of the Allies against Austro-Hungary and German South-West Africa fell in July, freeing men to fight in German East Africa and France.

militarist. In March, at a secret conference in London, Italy was promised extensive territories in the Tyrol, Dalmatia and Istria in the event of an Allied victory, and in May, she declared war on Austria. However, in one battle after another the Italians failed to take the Austrian bridgeheads on the River Isonzo, and the new belligerent was hardly to affect the course of the war in the rest of Europe.

At sea, the British had the best of an unimpressive action off the Dogger Bank. The Germans proclaimed a submarine blockade of the British Isles, and both sides set themselves to prevent supplies getting through to the enemy. This caused difficulties between Britain and the neutral USA. German-American tension became far more acute after a U-boat sank the *Lusitania*, a liner that was also carrying arms and munitions to Britain – 1,198 passengers died, including 139 Americans. The tension finally relaxed when the Germans declared that no liner would be sunk in future without prior warning and some provision for the passengers' safety.

In 1915, the Fokker fighter plane gave Germany temporary mastery of the air, the same year as Hugo Junkers produced the first all-metal aeroplane. The South Africans conquered German South-West Africa (now Namibia). D. W. Griffith's epic film *Birth of a Nation* was released. The Futurist poet Mayakovsky composed his poem *A Cloud in Trousers.* Somerset Maugham's *Of Human Bondage* and John Buchan's thriller *The Thirty-Nine Steps* appeared, as did D. H. Lawrence's *The Rainbow*, which then promptly disappeared after being pronounced obscene by a British judge.

Kobal Collection

D. W. Griffith's *Birth of a Nation* (1915)
(above) This three-hour epic recounts the intertwining stories of two familes caught up on opposite sides of the American Civil War. Originally titled The Clansman, *the film follows its source novel in praising the Ku Klux Klan and damning the southern black. The film sparked off race riots in several large cities in the United States and was banned in Europe for its racism.*

JOAN MIRÓ

1893-1983

Together with Picasso, Miró is perhaps the most versatile and influential of 20th-century artists. Although he was born into a family of craftsmen, his father frustrated his early ambitions to become a painter, forcing him to accept a job as a bookkeeper in Barcelona. As a result, Miró suffered a nervous breakdown, but it only strengthened his resolve. He left for Paris in 1919, where he met the avant-garde Surrealists.

Miró divided his time between France and Spain, and later America, where he executed murals for hotels and universities. His natural humour and love of anecdotal detail quickly popularized his work; but it also has a savage and macabre streak which was released by the shattering events of the Spanish Civil War and World War II. Like Picasso, Miró continued his artistic experiments into his old age.

The Modest Catalan

Miró's taciturn nature belied his profound imagination and creativity. A life of hard work, divided between Paris and the Catalan hills, produced unrivalled work which continues to inspire.

Joan Miró was born on 20 April 1893 in Barcelona. The family lived in the Pasaje del Crédito in the heart of the old city, where Miró's father Miguel ran a prosperous business as a jeweller and watchmaker. There was artisan talent on his mother's side too: Dolores Ferrá's father was a skilful cabinet maker. From the age of seven, Miró was sketching careful portraits and still-lifes, but Dolores and Miguel constantly frustrated his artistic ambitions.

Miró announced his intention to become a painter early on, but Miguel turned a deaf ear in spite of his son's abysmal performance at school. Miró showed a complete ineptitude for academic study and was known as 'fathead' by his fellow pupils. The pattern repeated itself in 1907, when Miró enrolled at La Lonja, the Barcelona school of Fine Arts where Picasso had studied 12 years earlier. He was soon dubbed a 'phenomenon of clumsiness'. But his tutor could see a spark of

originality and brilliance in his clumsy attempts, and each week, when Miguel called hoping to be assured of Miró's incompetence, he was told that one day, Miró would be a famous artist.

Miguel was unimpressed and in 1910, forced his son to accept a respectable job as a bookkeeper for a local drugstore. Miró dutifully obeyed, but it broke his spirit. The tedium of the work and the stifling of his creative energies brought on an appalling nervous depression, soon compounded by an attack of typhoid fever, and in desperation his parents sent him to recuperate at their farm near Montroig in the Catalan hills. The surrounding landscape made a lasting impression on the young artist.

Once back in Barcelona, Miró was no longer to be dissuaded from his chosen career. He joined Francisco Galí's liberal-minded art school and associated with the artists of the Sant Lluch circle, some of whom became lifelong friends, like Joseph

AISA

F. Catala-Roca

The young Miró
(left) Dressed for his First Communion, Miró looks neat but shy and already introspective, as friends always remembered him. He is probably about seven here, the same age that he began to sketch as a welcome relief from hated schoolwork.

A cultural centre
(below) Miró spent his youth in Barcelona, when it was the artistic centre of Spain. He painted for hours in the tiny room where he was born, and, unlike his compatriot Picasso, was rarely distracted by the bohemian nightlife of the city.

Inspiring scenery
(above) While convalescing at the family farm near Montroig, Miró was struck by the fertile landscape of the Catalan hills. 'When I set to work on a landscape I begin by loving it', he wrote. The area was a lifelong inspiration.

BARCELONA. 44 – Almacenes del Puerto y vista panoramica del Paseo de Colón.
44 – Havenaj Magazenoj kaj Promenejo de Kolumbo laŭ Panorama vidajo.

Jean-Loup Charmet

tiny studio where he worked at 45 rue Blomet, near Montparnasse, had broken window panes, and his rickety stove, picked up for 45 francs in the flea market, refused to work. He was so poor that he could only afford one proper lunch a week.

But there was consolation in the circle of intellectuals, poets and painters whom Miró met through his next-door neighbour, André Masson. Masson, Paul Eluard, Louis Aragon, Robert Desnos, Antonin Artaud and André Breton would frequently gather to discuss the ideas which Breton set down in the first Surrealist Manifesto of 1924. Miró was fascinated by their attempts to explore the subconscious, often through artificially induced means, and attended the meetings where the poet Desnos and the actor Artaud gave hysterical speeches in states of hallucination.

These experiments encouraged Miró to move away from the depiction of everyday reality in his own work, and to rely instead on his imagination and the hallucinatory forms and sensations he experienced through extreme hunger. He would sit for hours staring at the bare walls of his studio and sketching the strange shapes which appeared in front of his eyes. He did not take drugs himself, and he remained aloof from the internal squabbles

The influence of medieval masters
(below) The Romanesque chapels of Catalonia were decorated with colourful scenes, which Miró admired for their naivety and bold distortions.

Llorens Artigas. With his new bohemian acquaintances, Miró haunted the Barcelona cafés and nightclubs, but he shunned their dissipated lifestyle, indulging his fascination with the Spanish dancers only on paper. He was always the first to go home. More rewarding were his contacts with the avant-garde French artists and poets who travelled to Barcelona during the war years, and his discovery of the Fauve and Cubist paintings at Joseph Dalmau's gallery.

THE LURE OF PARIS

Dalmau offered Miró his first one-man exhibition in 1918. The public response was very poor but the artist was undeterred, knowing that success and the international recognition he already dreamed of could only be found in Paris. The French capital had a magnetic appeal for him, and in 1919, when Paris was at last safe, after the war, he made his first trip there. Over the next few years, winters in Paris and quiet summers at Montroig became his regular working pattern.

Paris was a stimulating but ruthless city for obscure and impoverished artists. One of the first things Miró did when he arrived was to look up his fellow Spaniard, Picasso. Picasso bought a self-portrait from Miró to encourage his new friend, but sales were hard to come by, and Miró's financial situation was perilous. His parents provided ludicrously small sums intended to convey their utter disapproval of his activities. The

Key Dates

1893 born in Barcelona

1910 accepts job as a bookkeeper

1911 suffers nervous breakdown; determines to become a painter

1919 visits Paris and meets Picasso

1928 trip to Holland

1929 marries Pilar Juncosa

1936 Spanish Civil War breaks out

1940 escapes France to Palma

1942 returns to Barcelona

1944 ceramic experiments with Artigas

1947 visits America

1956 builds large studio at Calamayor

1970 ceramic mural for Barcelona airport

1983 dies on Christmas Day

Museo di Arte Catalana, Barcelona

Miró and Surrealism

In Paris during the 1920s, Miró associated with the avant-garde Surrealist poets and painters who had gathered around a charismatic spokesman, André Breton. Breton greatly admired Miró and later wrote 'the tumultuous entrance of Miró in 1924 marks an important point in the development of Surrealist art'. Miró attended the sessions when members of the group experimented with drugs and alcohol to induce states of hallucination and free their minds from conscious control. He formed close friendships with many of them, living next door to Arp, Ernst and Magritte in rue Tourlaque, but he disassociated himself from the group when they became increasingly involved in politics and the Communist party in the 1930s.

Tristan Tzara
(left) Tzara was a poet and friend of the Surrealists who initiated a revolt against conventional values in art. Miró illustrated some of his poems, including 'L'arbre des voyageurs'.

The Minotaure
(above) Miró designed this cover for Minotaure, the magazine which was a forum for the avant-garde, embracing literature, archaeology and music, as well as the fine arts.

of the group, but he began to exhibit with the Surrealists, showing his new 'dream paintings' at Pierre Loeb's gallery and the Galerie Surréaliste.

A contract with the dealer Jacques Viot enabled him to keep afloat financially, and Viot found him a studio in Montmartre at 22 rue Tourlaque, where his new neighbours included Max Ernst, René Magritte and Jean Arp. Miró struck up close friendships with Arp and Ernst in particular, but he was rarely to be seen with them at the Café Cyrano in Place Pigalle, or the Café de la Place Blanche where the Surrealists gathered to discuss theories and write manifestos, or organize exhibitions.

Miró was working compulsively, and becoming increasingly secretive about his own paintings. He kept them all turned face to the wall, away from the curious gaze of Ernst, who worked in the

studio above. One night Ernst and some drunken friends stormed his studio, sorted through all the canvases to discover their secrets, and then strung Miró up in a hangman's noose and started to squeeze the life out of him, pulling hard on the rope. The sober Miró somehow managed to extricate himself from the noose and went into terrified hiding for three days.

But Ernst's drunken revelries never soured his friendship with Miró or their admiration for each other, and occasionally they worked together, both agreeing to design the costumes and scenery for Diaghilev's ballet, *Romeo and Juliet*. Breton, the dogmatic leader of the Surrealist group, violently disapproved of their involvement in what he considered to be the bourgeois and frivolous world of ballet. He staged a demonstration in the theatre on the opening night, and denounced them in his

'assassinate painting' which had been 'decadent since the cave age'.

Miró's new troubled state of mind had nothing to do with his personal fortunes. In 1929, he married Pilar Juncosa and settled down to a perfectly happy married life. Two years later, his daughter Dolores was born. But the 1930s held horrors in store which Miró could not disguise in his art of those years.

Miró was now spending more time in Spain, increasingly alienated from the Surrealists and their political squabbles over joining the Communist party. But he was acutely sensitive to the threat of Fascism which was terrorizing the people of his own country. His pictures, which he called 'peintures sauvages', were menaced by violent distortions and aggressive monsters and a terrible sense of impending catastrophe. Miró was anticipating war.

THE OUTBREAK OF CIVIL WAR

In 1936, civil war broke out in Spain, and Miró was forced to return to Paris. The following year he designed the poster *Aidez Espagne* (p.91) to be sold for one franc to help the Spaniards in their struggle for liberty. It showed a Catalan peasant shaking a swollen and defiant clenched fist. He also painted *The Reaper* for the Spanish Republican Government, to hang next to Picasso's *Guernica* at the International Exhibition in Paris, and the dramatic *Still-Life with an Old Shoe*, in which an apple, symbolizing Spain, is aggressively pierced

magazine, *La Révolution Surréaliste*. But Miró had never bowed to Breton's intellectual dogmas or his authority, preferring to keep his distance when it suited him.

In 1928, Miró visited Holland, where the bourgeois interiors depicted by the 17th-century Dutch painters, and Vermeer in particular, intrigued him. He brought back postcard reproductions and used them for a series of paintings, including *Dutch Interior I* (p.85), in which he distorted and rearranged the contents of the originals with a great sense of humour. But soon afterwards, Miró abandoned the easy charm of these pictures and started on a series of collages and constructions made from bits and pieces of debris, often salvaged from dustbins; unpleasant objects and materials put together for their shock value. He declared that he was going to

Spanish Civil War
(above) When civil war broke out in Spain in 1936 there was enormous support abroad for the Republicans fighting Franco. Many artists including Miró, who was shattered by the butchery, designed propaganda posters to help.

The artist in America
(right) After the Second World War, Miró found a new lease of life in America, inspired by its energy and optimism.

watching the soft light filtering through the stained-glass windows. In 1942, he took his family back to Barcelona. His lasting anger at the senseless ravages of war surfaced in some horrifying lithographs – *The Barcelona Suite* – but he also found a vital creative outlet in ceramic experiments with his childhood friend, Artigas.

By now his international reputation had grown, particularly in America where his work was shown regularly at the Pierre Matisse gallery. He made the first of many trips to America in 1947, invited by the Directors of the Terrace Hilton Hotel in Cincinnati to paint an enormous mural for their Gourmet Restaurant. This coincided perfectly with a new desire to communicate with the public and express himself on a huge scale.

Miró also visited New York, where the exciting pace of the city and the youthful optimism of the people gave him a new lease of life and a desire to pick up with old friends, ending a long period of

by the bayonet-like prongs of a fork.

But soon the problems of Spain were eclipsed by the shattering events of World War II. Paris was no longer safe, and Miró found a temporary retreat in a small cottage, 'Le Clos des Sansonnets', near Varengeville-sur-mer in Normandy, not far from the house his friend Braque had built for himself a few years before. 'I was very depressed', Miró later wrote. 'I believed in an inevitable victory for Nazism, and that all that we love and that gives us our reason for living was sunk for ever in the abyss.' Only a few months later, German bombardments threatened Varengeville and Miró was on the run once more, heading south through Paris and arriving in Spain just a few days before the Germans marched into the French capital.

Miró settled temporarily in Majorca, finding some respite in peaceful hours spent at the cathedral of Palma, listening to organ recitals and

A Majorcan retreat
(above) When the Germans took Paris, Miró escaped to Palma and the peaceful atmosphere of its cathedral where he listened to Bach and Mozart and studied the sculptures. He eventually bought two houses and built a studio amongst the olive groves of nearby Calamayor.

International fame
(right) Miró could hardly keep up with the demands of worldwide exhibitions. Here he and his wife are greeted at an opening.

Art for the masses

In 1938, Miró wrote 'I'd like to get beyond easel painting, which in my opinion pursues a petty aim, and find ways of getting closer, in terms of painting, to the broad mass of human beings who have always been in my thoughts.' He wanted his art to be accessible and murals were the perfect means of expressing himself on a large scale and communicating with the public. He liked to feel he was fulfilling a social function like the Romanesque artists and even the cave painters, and that his primitive magical forms could appeal to the dynamic modern societies of France, Spain and especially America.

The Terrace Plaza (Hilton) Hotel, Cincinnati
(right) This brightly coloured decorative painting was Miró's first mural commission, executed in 1947 for the restaurant of the hotel.

introspection and detachment. On his return to Paris in 1948, after eight years' absence, he was given a hero's welcome and an exhibition of his work at the Galerie Maeght was a resounding commercial success.

Miró was soon weighed under with monumental commissions from the Americans, the French and the Spanish, including paintings and ceramic murals for Harvard University, the Solomon R. Guggenheim Museum, the ceramic *Wall of the Sun* and *Wall of the Moon* for Unesco, Paris, a large monument for the Cervantes Gardens in Barcelona and, as late as 1970, an enormous ceramic mural for display at Barcelona airport.

To work more effectively for the public, Miró increasingly devoted his energies to lithographs, engravings, etchings and popular crafts – ceramic vases and dishes, for example – all of which were much cheaper than easel paintings and could be widely disseminated. In 1954, he was awarded the Venice Biennale Grand Prize for engraving, and from the hands of President Eisenhower he received the Grand International Prize of the Guggenheim Foundation.

THE FOUNDATION MAEGHT

To cope with the flood of commissions and the time-consuming organization of regular world-wide exhibitions, the Foundation Maeght was set up in his honour at St Paul de Vence in 1964. Ceaselessly energetic, Miró spent the last two decades of his life rushing from Montroig to his printers in Paris, back to Artigas's kilns in the mountains of Gallifa, and, if he needed to work alone, to the enormous studio specially built for him by José Luis Sert among the terraces and olive trees of Calamayor near Palma. This was the only large studio he had ever owned, but of which he

had always dreamed while working in the cramped conditions of his Paris studios and his tiny room in the Pasaje del Crédito, where he remembered banging his head against the walls when things got too much for him.

Right up until his death on 25 December 1983, Miró worked exhaustively, learning the techniques of monotype when he was 84, and at 86 producing his first stained-glass windows for the Foundation Maeght. But with an output and a reputation rivalled only by that of Picasso, the frail, modest old man remained undazzled by his glory to the end.

Unfailing inspiration
(below) Miró was remarkably creative and versatile in his old age, constantly experimenting with pottery, sculpture, stained glass, monotype and lithography as well as painting. He enjoyed collaborative work but remained a recluse, happiest working in his last studio at Calamayor.

Marc Eiboud/John Hillelson Agency

Cincinnati Art Museum

Roguish Humour

Through patient effort, Miró evolved an art of beguiling freshness and spontaneity, developing a highly personal language of signs and symbols and displaying his savage delight in the absurd.

At the beginning of the century, Barcelona, capital of Catalonia, was the cultural centre of Spain. It was here that Miró discovered the works of the Post-Impressionists, the Fauves and the Cubists which helped to shape his early style. But it was Catalonia's mountainous landscape where Miró's family came from that was his greatest inspiration. In his early 'realist' paintings, he recorded every detail of this landscape with scrupulous attention and devotion. 'What interests me above all', he wrote to a friend, 'are the tiles on the roof, the calligraphy of a tree, leaf by leaf and branch by branch, blade of grass by blade of grass.' While he was working on *The Farm* in 1921-2 – a tribute to his family house in Montroig – he used to take clods of earth and grasses with him in his suitcase when he travelled to Paris, so that the precise details would not escape him.

But there was also a strong element of fantasy in Miró's character, which attracted him to the less realistic work of the early Romanesque painters who decorated the old Catalan chapels with frescoes of simple, brightly-coloured figures, using distortion and a hieratic scale for symbolic or emotional effects. He also admired the stocky painted plaster figures made by local artisans for their lack of artistic pretension. Such things appealed to him for their naive humour and honesty, and the tricks of distortion and of depicting important things much larger were later assimilated into his own work.

In Paris, Miró was encouraged to develop his

Collection, The Museum of Modern Art

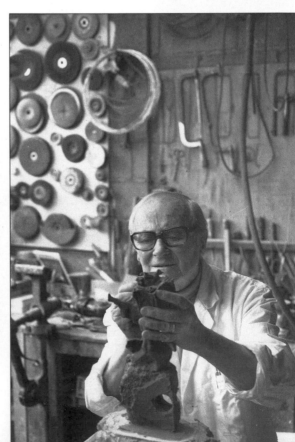

The Beautiful Bird Revealing the Unknown to a Pair of Lovers
(left) Between 1940 and 1941, Miró painted a series of 23 small gouache 'Constellations', in which shapes and dots of colour multiply .

© ADAGP 1988

Henri Cartier-Bresson/Magnum

religious and magic sense of things, which is that of primitive peoples'. He developed his new figures by a process of simplification, a stripping away of unnecessary details. 'Showing all the details', he said, 'would deprive them of that imaginary life that enlarges everything.'

The same figures – Catalan peasants, women and birds, ladders, stars and strange nocturnal creatures – appear over and over again in his work. The ladder, for example, was part of the familiar clutter around the Montroig farmhouse, but gradually it became transformed in Miró's paintings into a symbol of escape, often leading into a night sky as in *Dog Barking at the Moon* (left). Woman was usually portrayed as Mother Earth, 'to whom Miró always offers his devotion': a symbol of fecundity as she is often shown in primitive ethnic sculptures. And the bird, like the ladder, represents the freedom of the spirit and an escape from mundane everyday reality. Other shapes and hieroglyphs are not so easy to interpret, sometimes being there just to satisfy Miró's sense of balanced composition, but they all contribute to the haunting fascination of his work. 'It is signs that have no precise meaning that provoke a magic sense', he believed. Sometimes, these eccentric symbols are reminiscent of Chinese or Japanese written characters, and Miró's paintings become a playful form of calligraphy.

Miró felt free to distort and rearrange as his imagination dictated, and to place anatomical forms – arms, heads, breasts, hands and feet – and other signs in comical juxtapositions. Some of his

Lithographic designs

(below) Miró designed this striking poster to publicize his book 'The Lizard with Golden Feathers', which he illustrated with lithographic plates and calligraphy.

Dog Barking at the Moon

(above) The ladder was one of Miró's favourite symbols, providing a link between earth and sky, and a means of escape to the spiritual plane.

Exploring sculpture

(left) Miró only began to sculpt when he was in his fifties, although his interest in the medium had been stimulated many years earlier by his teacher Galí. Galí had blindfolded Miró and then placed objects in his hands for him to draw, in an exercise which was designed to help Miró 'to "see" form' and to develop a feeling for solid mass.

imaginative faculties by the Surrealist poets and artists that he met. Fascinated by their experiments with summoning up the unconscious through states of hallucination, he would sit for hours in his studio capturing the strange sensations and forms he experienced when hallucinating himself through extreme hunger. The artistic freedom of this method was vital to his creative development: from the early 1920s onwards, Miró no longer used space and colour in a realistic way to depict everyday objects, and the forms that appeared in his paintings became a personal language of signs and symbols.

SIMPLIFYING FORMS

Miró's Catalan peasants became stick-life figures, for example, recognizable by their attributes: a Phrygian cap and a pipe perhaps, or a wedge-shaped hunter's knife and gun. Many of Miró's humorous figures look naive and unsophisticated, like children's doodles, and he was deliberately trying to evolve an art that would stimulate basic sensations of humour, fear, excitement and passion in the spectator; to 'rediscover the

Private Collection

paintings, like *Carnival of Harlequin* (pp.88-9), are very lighthearted and humorous, as if Miró took a childish delight in arranging his toys, but his forms have also been described as 'torture instruments'.

During the 1930s and the war years, and particularly in the *Barcelona Suite* of lithographs, Miró created a nightmare world of vicious grossly distorted monsters. His women sprouted ugly spikes of hair, claw-like nails and their gaping mouths are filled with jagged fangs. Both his males and females, often attacking each other, were given enormous sexual organs. Distressed and disturbed by political events, Miró was showing man in all his bestiality and cruelty, indulging his most destructive instinctual drives and the coarser aspect of his humour.

Miró had no respect for conventional aesthetic standards. Apart from the content of his work, he often chose to use the meanest of materials, making collages and sculptures out of cardboard and old sacking, lengths of rope, rusty nails and bed springs, broken crockery and endless bits and pieces picked up on his walks. Often these objects were the inspiration he needed to spark a composition, supplying 'the shock which suggests the form just as cracks in a wall suggested shapes to Leonardo'. Sometimes, just a splotch of colour on a canvas, a dribble of turpentine or an escaping thread would do the same.

LASTING INFLUENCE

Miro's influence on 20th-century artists has been enormous. His fascination with textures and his free, spontaneous creations inspired the Tachiste painters and 'action' painters like Jackson Pollock, while his strange, naive characters were taken up by the Art Brut painters after World War II. His enormously varied output, covering painting, sculpture, ceramics, collages, etchings, engravings and lithographs, remains a continuing source of inspiration to modern artists.

COMPARISONS

Dutch Anecdotal Detail

Dutch 17th-century artists often depicted humorous genre scenes, like *The Cat's Dancing Lesson*. Their love of anecdote and symbolic detail appealed to Miró, and especially to his sense of the absurd. Just as Jan Steen painted the woman playing music to a cat, Miró's guitar player in *Dutch Interior I* (opposite) has enticed a fluttering bat into the room. Miró also has his own language of symbols. He gives his guitarist a prominent ear as a humorous tribute to the musician's sensitivity.

Rijksmuseum, Amsterdam

Rijksmuseum, Amsterdam

Jan Steen (1626-1679) **The Cat's Dancing Lesson**
(left) Steen's painting inspired Miró's Dutch Interior II, in the Peggy Guggenheim Collection.

Hendrick Sorgh (1610/11-1670) **The Lutanist**
(above) The minor objects in Sorgh's painting serve as symbolic clues to the romantic narrative.

Dutch Interior I

In 1928, Miró paid a brief visit to Holland, where he was intrigued by the detailed realism of Dutch 17th-century genre paintings in Amsterdam's Rijksmuseum. He returned to Paris with a few postcard reproductions of the pictures he had seen, from which he painted his own series of 'Dutch Interiors'. *Dutch Interior I* was based on Hendrick Sorgh's *Lutanist* of 1661 (opposite). Miró, however, transformed the original with the medieval logic of the Romanesque Catalan artists, using a hieratic scale to paint important things large and unimportant things small – and sometimes removing them altogether. Instead of the lyricism of Sorgh's picture, Miró's 'Dutch Interior' has a frenzied, dancing rhythm.

Departing from reality
(left and detail above) Miró takes outrageous liberties with Sorgh's painting. The dog, the table, the cat and the view of Amsterdam through the window all remain, although they have undergone radical transformations, but the woman has virtually disappeared and Miró has added whimsical details like the frog chasing an insect, the kitchen knife peeling an apple of its own accord, the bat entranced by the music and, on the right, a large dirty footprint.

1928/36⅛" × 28¾/¹ oil on canvas/Mrs Simon Guggenheim Fund

Collection, The Museum of Modern Art, New York

'It is essential to have your feet firmly planted on the soil in order to leap into the air.'

Miró

TRADEMARKS

Playful Forms

Under the influence of Surrealism, Miró allowed his hand to be guided by his imagination, inventing cryptic signs and fantastic forms which delight us with their playful exuberance.

Gallery

Miró was an extremely versatile, inventive and prolific artist. His career does not show any steady evolution of style, but rather an unquenchable thirst for experiment, a tireless ability to absorb and transform new influences, and an imaginative response to the varied qualities of the differing materials with which he worked. Miró himself commented on the element of uncertainty and lack of premeditation in his creative processes, writing 'It is difficult for me to speak of my painting, for it is always born in a state of hallucination, provoked by some shock or other, objective or subjective, for which I am entirely unresponsible', and although he later modified the views in this statement (made in 1933) it gives an indication of the fascinating unpredictability of his work. It ranges from the loving detail of Kitchen Garden with a Donkey to the daringly empty abstract forms of Blue III, from the mischievous playfulness of Harlequin's Carnival to the bitter anger of Aidez Espagne. And Miró's genius was such that he was just as happy working on a fairly small scale in the medium of lithography as he was creating huge decorative murals. Both satisfied his urge to create an art which belonged to the public at large, by-passing the exclusivity of the museums.

Kitchen Garden with a Donkey *1918*
25½″ × 27½″ Moderne Museet, Stockholm

This is one of the first paintings in which Miró worked in the style to which a friend gave the name 'detallista', characterized by great attention to detail and sharpness of focus from foreground to background. The overall feeling, however, is not naturalistic, for the stylized forms and the rhythmic patterns made by, for example, the lines of cultivation and the branches against the sky, produce an effect somewhat like a complex stage set. Miró holds together the diverse elements with consummate skill, and the bright colours and clear forms convey with great vividness the heat of his native Catalonia.

oil on canvas/Room of Contemporary Art Fund, 1940

Carnival of Harlequin *(1924-25)*
26″ × 36⅝″ Albright-Knox Art Gallery,
Buffalo, New York

In 1938, Miró wrote an article in which he described the genesis of this painting, one of his most famous works and one of the first in which he revealed his unmistakable personal style. At the time, he was experiencing a period of great hardship and he wrote 'For Harlequin's Carnival I made many drawings in which I expressed my hallucinations brought on by hunger. I came home at night without having dined and noted my sensations on paper.' A room with a window and table are indicated and they belong more or less to the everyday world, but after that Miró's imagination takes over. A bizarre assembly of insect-like creatures play, dance and make music, one of them having the suggestion of a human face with a ridiculous moustache. It has been said that Miró's vision in this painting is essentially childlike, but the skill with which he unifies the flow of movement and incident is that of a highly sophisticated artist.

Portrait of Mistress Mills in 1750 *(1929)*
46″ × 35¼″ Collection, The Museum of Modern Art, New York

*In 1929, Miró made a series of four 'Imaginary Portraits' based on
paintings of the past; this one was inspired by an engraving of a portrait
by the minor English painter George Engleheart (1752-1829). The
head and neck of the sitter are reduced to little more than ciphers
underneath the dominating form of her broad-brimmed hat.*

Aidez Espagne *(1937)*
9¾″ × 7⅝″ Collection, The Museum of Modern Art, New York

*Miró felt despair at the Spanish Civil War and he produced this
silk-screen print to be sold in aid of relief for his native country – the
price of one franc is a bold part of the design. The powerfully conceived
figure is shown clenching a massive fist in the Loyalist salute and the
inscription tells of the 'immense creative resources' of the people of Spain.*

Inverted Personages *1949*
31¼″ × 21½″ Kunstmuseum, Basle

*On his return to Paris from America, Miró produced a great number
of paintings in two complementary styles – which have been described
as 'slow paintings' and 'quick paintings'. This light-hearted work
belongs to the former category, with its careful delineation of shapes
and forms and its dense application of bright primary colour.*

Women and Birds in the Moonlight *1949*
32″ × 26″ Tate Gallery, London

*Miró was haunted by the theme of the night, the time for dreams,
silence and solitude and for mystic communion with the stars. His
nocturnal landscapes are often inhabited by women, who sway in the
moonlight, and 'birds of the night' – symbols of the flight of the
spirit from the waking consciousness of day.*

© ADAGP 1988/oil on canvas/Mrs Simon Guggenheim Fund

Mural Painting: Barcelona *(1950-51)*
74¾" × 233¾" Collection, The Museum of Modern Art, New York

Miró's decorative style was well adapted to work on a large scale and he liked the challenge of painting for a specific public place. This mural – almost 20 feet wide – was painted for the dining room of the Harkness Commons building at Harvard University, at the suggestion of the great architect Walter Gropius. Miró executed the painting in Barcelona and it was installed in 1951, but in the next few years it was found that it was deteriorating and Miró proposed that a ceramic version should be substituted. Miró described the subject cryptically as 'of a muralistic and poetic significance', but some commentators have suggested that it shows a bullfight scene. In the centre of the composition is a bull, with two enormous black horns and the enlarged sexual organs so often seen in Miró's work.

Joan Miró

Blue III *1961*
106¼″ × 139¾″ Pierre Matisse Gallery, New York

This is the last in a series of three similar paintings (Blue I, II and III) that Miró executed in 1961. It illustrates the great range of Miró's imagination, for whereas many of his best-known works are comparatively small and crowded with restlessly moving incident and detail, this one is huge and serenely sparse. It has links with some of his more characteristic works, however, in the strange, amoeba-like form that trails across the blue void, suggesting the immensity and mysteries of the universe. The blue itself – one of Miró's favourite colours – was described by his early champion, René Gaffé, as 'a savage blue, insolent, electric, which sufficed by itself to make the canvas vibrate'.

97

Lithograph from 'Art for Research' *1969*
30″ × 21½″ Private Collection

*Miró was one of the greatest graphic artists the 20th century has seen,
excelling particularly at lithography – the making of prints from a
specially prepared stone surface. This is one of a series of ten prints by
Miró and nine other artists published as a portfolio to benefit the Swiss
Centre for Clinical Research on Cancer.*

Lithograph from 'Seers' *1970*
20″ × 26″ Private Collection

*This is one of a series of six lithographs entitled 'Seers'. A seer is a
prophet or someone who has the power to see into the future, and the
handprints here allude to the idea of palm-reading. The bright colours,
spattered background and whirling shapes suggest the state of ecstasy
which the seer must enter in order to transcend earthly experience.*

The Spanish Civil War

Though the Civil War of 1936-39 was largely a Spanish affair, to the world outside it came to represent a universal struggle between the philosophies of socialism and fascism.

When civil war broke out in 1936 in Spain, the country had been wracked by violent internal dissent for almost 150 years. Alternating liberal and conservative governments had been unable to establish a stable regime with or without a monarch. In 1931, Spain declared itself a republic for the second time when Alphonso XIII was sent to France in exile.

However, the liberal government – a coalition of largely left-wing parties which brought in sweeping changes to make Spain 'a democratic republic of workers of all classes' – was soon buffeted by discontent from all sides.

Despised by the traditionally-minded forces of the army, landowners and the Church, the government was not in a good position to defend

Roger Viollet

Fundación Figueras, Barcelona

The call to arms
(left) This Nationalist poster – incorporating the Falangist red arrow emblem – urges soldiers to take up arms in the name of 'the fatherland, bread and justice'.

The Generalissimo
(above) Franco – seen here talking to the family of Primo de Rivera – was chosen by his fellow generals in 1936 to be Commander of the Nationalist forces.

itself. It was an unstable coalition and some of its members were more idealistic than politically aware. Neither did the world slump of the 1930s, which added to Spain's endemic depression, help the liberal government's well-intentioned efforts to bring Spain out of centuries of feudal repression.

Socialists and Communists also criticized the government – though they basically supported it – for not going far enough in its reforms. And supporters of Spain's huge left-wing anarcho-syndicalist movement took to the streets and fields in violent protest against what they perceived as a feeble, do-little administration.

Meanwhile, a group of leading army officers –

Popperfoto

The defence of Catalonia
(right) *The Republican government had been sympathetic towards the Catalan separatist movement, and had granted Catalonia autonomy and its own flag in 1932. These privileges came under attack when the Right seized power in 1936, causing widespread anger and resentment. This poster, with its banner calling 'Brothers to the Front', was issued by the left-wing Catalan party Esquerra as part of its effort to create a mass mobilization against Franco's oppressive government.*

Storming the Alcázar
(below) *In September 1936 loyal Republican forces recaptured Toledo except for the castle of the Alcázar, where rebel troops were entrenched. Their long but doomed resistance against great odds became a set-piece of Nationalist propaganda.*

including Spain's youngest general, Francisco Franco – believed that their country was about to go the revolutionary way of Soviet Russia. These military men bitterly resented the removal of privileges, such as the army's exemption from the jurisdiction of the civil courts – and they had powerful allies. In the country, landowners baulked at government reforms to improve the lot of landless peasants, and in the towns and cities, men of property lamented the introduction of minimum wage agreements and a statutory eight-hour day. Politically-minded Catholics objected to the government's assault on the traditional role of the Church in Spanish society, and there were many who disapproved of the government's active sympathy with the regionalist aspirations of the Basques and the Catalans.

Elections in 1933 ousted the government and, under a new, much more right-wing regime, virtually all the progressive legislation of the first administration was repealed. As success for the Right increased its confidence and militancy, attitudes on the Left hardened too.

In 1934, the atmosphere of crisis intensified and the Socialists revolted. Nearly every prominent leftist leader in Spain was arrested and imprisoned, while the great mass of the rural poor groaned under the government's agrarian policies which maintained the almost feudal, pre-Republican situation. Finally, in February 1936, the government fell and was replaced by a coalition of left and moderate political forces – a Popular Front.

But right-wing monarchists and conservatives were not content to accept defeat. Top army officers began sinister consultations with leading right-wing politicians. On 17 July 1936, the restive generals made a declaration of their intent – the *pronunciamento*. The next day, all the garrisons in Spain joined the revolt. Franco turned for help to like-minded European leaders – Hitler, Mussolini and Portugal's Salazar. Franco had many ideas in common with Hitler and Mussolini, and was supported by Spain's own Fascist organization, the Falange, which he headed after 1937.

On the other side, the Soviet Union sent some fighter planes to help the beleaguered Republican government which sent gold reserves to buy Russian arms. But Russian support was less substantial than that offered by Italy and Germany to Franco.

In the first six months, the 'Nationalist' rebels carried all before them in the west and south of Spain. Apart from the advantage of surprise and military strength, they benefited from the unified leadership of 'Generalissimo' Franco. By the end of 1936, he had established himself as Chief of the Spanish State with the full blessing of the Church. Franco's first acts were to repeal the Republican liberal laws on divorce, Catalan autonomy and agrarian reform, leaving people with no doubts as to the character of the Spain he was fighting for.

Whatever the blunders and shortcomings of the Republican government, the Nationalists had underestimated its popular support. Though poorly equipped and chaotically organized, peasants and workers, intellectuals and many ordinary soldiers, Basques and Catalans, all rallied to its cause. But the bickering Republican government, now including Communists, Socialists and even anarchists, could not meet the challenge. It lurched from crisis to crisis while

Exodus
(left) Aurelio Arteta's painting conveys the suffering and resignation of a group of civilian refugees. Fighting forced half a million people to abandon their homes and belongings and seek asylum abroad.

Refugee soldiers
(above) Thousands of Republicans were executed in the months following Franco's victory. Many soldiers, fearing for their lives, fled over the border to the south of France, where they were put into internment camps.

Franco acquired half of Spain.

Spain's ferocious civil war was stained by atrocities on both sides. Many of the early Nationalist gains were made only after the wholesale slaughter of dissidents. Enraged, the Republicans and anti-clericals took summary vengeance on members of the upper classes, and an estimated 5000 priests were killed in cold blood. And, as with most wars, real criminals took advantage of the turmoil to generate more violence and bloodshed.

Meanwhile, the governments of Western democracies like Britain and France pursued a policy of non-intervention in the war.

However, as refugees poured over the Pyrenees only to be thrown into camps, individual consciences were stirred. Some arms found their way to the Republic via France and left-wing groups – International Brigades, consisting mainly of Communists, trade unionists and intellectuals such as George Orwell and Ernest Hemingway – were formed across Europe and in America to fight against the Nationalists. Though they were to sustain heavy casualties, these volunteers helped prevent early victory for Franco.

At the end of 1936, Franco's conquests included the largest grain-producing areas and the length of

Joan Miró

Centro Internacional de la Historia, Barcelona

the Portuguese border. But when he tried to drive a wedge through the remaining Republican territory to reach Madrid, he failed. The International Brigades based at Madrid defeated his Italian allies at Guadalajara. Thwarted, Franco turned his attention to the northern Basque provinces, and here he was more successful.

In April 1937, the Basque capital of Guernica was subjected to saturation bombing by planes from Hitler's Condor legion. The ancient town was devastated and at least a thousand women, men and children were killed, with many more injured. The massacre at Guernica shocked the world and in their guilty anxiety, the Nationalists tried to conceal what they had done. But eye-witness reports soon appeared in newspapers in a dozen countries, and from his exile in Paris, Pablo Picasso began his painting of *Guernica*.

Slowly but surely, the Nationalists, by superiority of military skill and armaments, gained the upper hand. By August 1938, Franco had broken through government territory to reach the Mediterranean. The Republican government was still frustrated in its attempts to obtain supplies from sympathetic countries and heard its death knell tolled when the Russians cut off their limited aid in 1939. After repeated heavy bombing, Barcelona fell in 1939 and then Madrid capitulated. Backed by intrigue and internal dissent, the forces of the legitimate government collapsed.

Franco insisted on unconditional surrender and his victory was not magnanimous. According to conservative estimates, as many people were put to death after the war as had been killed during it: Spain's ordeal had cost a million lives and caused incalculable material damage.

Fight for independence
(above) Republican propaganda often portrayed the war as a battle against foreign invaders. This poster proclaims 'Spain fights for its independence, for peace and solidarity among all peoples'.

The Madrid Massacre
(right) At the beginning of the war Madrid was firmly under Republican control, but the right-wing military rebelled in July 1936. The uprising was quelled after two days of street fighting during which the Republicans forced their way into the Montana Barracks and massacred everyone.

Popperfoto

A Year in the Life 1925

In 1925, while Miró and other Surrealists were putting on their first exhibition in Paris, European peace seemed secure and trust was placed in the authority of the League of Nations. But, during this year, Adolf Hitler published his belligerent ideas in *Mein Kampf* which were ultimately to lead to War.

At the first Surrealist Exhibition, held in Paris in 1925, the works of Miró, Picasso and Ernst asserted the primacy of the unconscious whereas in world affairs it seemed that reason might yet triumph. Germany, burdened by reparations and plunged into chaos by hyper-inflation, had been rescued by the 1924 Dawes Plan and, with the help of huge American loans, was making an economic recovery. Under the guidance of Gustav Stresemann, she also began to be accepted by her wartime enemies.

However, international security was not easily achieved. The Geneva Protocol, put before the League of Nations in October 1924 by the British Labour Prime Minister Ramsey MacDonald, proposed by system of arbitration to end conflicts between nations. But it foundered on opposition from the

Gustav Stresemann
(right) The Locarno Conference of 1925 was an attempt by the European powers, led by France and Britain, to effect a reconciliation with Stresemann's Germany whereby western borders were guaranteed and mutual assistance was invoked against a possible Soviet threat. The treaty, signed in December was violated in 1936 by Hitler's occupation of the Rhineland.

The Druze Rebellion
(below) In 1921 General Gourand invaded Syria with a camel-equipped force to impose a French mandatory régime which backed the traditionally Francophile Christians at the expense of the predominantly moslem population. In 1925 the Druze rose in violent rebellion, forming an alliance with nationalists in Damascus.

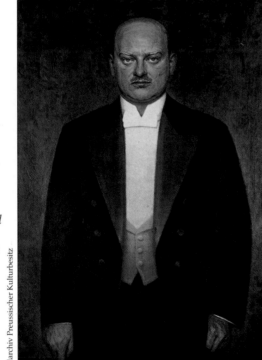

Bildarchiv Preussischer Kulturbesitz

Giancarlo Costa

Dominions; a French Canadian politician pointed out complacently that, 'We live in a fireproof house, far from inflammable materials.' In March 1925, Stanley Baldwin's newly elected Conservative government rejected the Protocol, which was then dropped.

THE LEAGUE OF NATIONS

Nonetheless, the League of Nations scored some real successes in 1925. Arrangements were made to control the opium trade and arms dealing; and when Greece attacked Bulgaria after border clashes, the League intervened to settle the dispute and extracted a fine from the Greeks.

In Europe, the failure of the Geneva Protocol was largely made good as a result of German proposals which were elaborated into the Locarno treaties. The European powers collectively guaranteed Germany's existing borders with most of her neighbours, and this, together with a set of arbitration agreements and the formation of Franco-Polish and Franco-Czechoslovak alliances, quieted French fears and seemed to ensure peace in Europe. The new atmosphere of international conciliation lasted until the 1929 Depression disrupted the entire political and economic system.

Germany's Weimar Republic was actually strengthened by a presidential election won by Paul von Hindenburg, the most prestigious wartime military leader. Though a conservative and monarchist, Hindenburg proved willing to accept republican institutions and so conferred respectability on them. The Nazi-

Soviet cinema

(left) Sergei Eisenstein's celebrated film The Battleship Potemkim *was derived, together with* Strike, *from an immense eight-episode project on the events of Russia's 1905 revolution. Influenced by his study of Japanese art, Futurism and the grandiosity of D. W. Griffith's epic film* Intolerance *(1916), Eisenstein succeeded in creating a visual and propagandist masterpiece in which scenes and individual shots have symbolic value as a reflection of the revolution as a whole. The Odessa steps sequence in which soldiers fire on the populace as they acclaim the mutineering sailors of the Potemkin is still celebrated as a cinematic tour de force.*

The Great Gatsby

(below) Francis Scott Fitzgerald made his literary debut at the age of 24 with This Side of Paradise *(1920), a novel which immediately launched him as the spokesman of the 'Jazz Age'. In 1925 he published* The Great Gatsby *(a still from the 1974 film of the same name is shown here), which charted the rise to wealth of Jay Gatsby, bootlegger, and his deep but blind love for Daisy, a glamorous and selfish married woman. The story ends in tragedy: Fitzgerald's celebration of the hectic excess of the 'Bright Young Things' with their wild parties and new found freedom, was always tempered with an objective eye and a good measure of cynicism.*

backed candidate, General Ludendorff, polled a derisory 210,000 votes. Peace and returning prosperity seemed to have dashed the hopes of agitators such as the Nazi leader Adolf Hitler. He was still on parole after his early release from prison (he had received a five-year sentence for his part in the 1923 'Beer Hall putsch' in Bavaria). The first volume of his book *Mein Kampf* was published in the summer of 1925 and set out explicitly the policies he was later to implement as Fuehrer of the Third Reich. An initial failure, by 1939 it was to sell over 5,200,000 copies in 11 languages.

1925 was also the year when Mrs Nellie Ross of Wyoming became the first woman state governor in the USA. Skirts were being worn just below the knee and were getting shorter. In Turkey, Mustapha Kemal banned polygamy and the wearing of the fez. At the celebrated 'Monkey Trial' in Tennessee, John A. Scopes was indicted for violating state laws by teaching Darwin's theory of evolution.

On the cultural front, 1925 saw the publication of Scott Fitzgerald's *The Great Gatsby*, John Dos Passos's *Manhattan Transfer* and Virginia Woolf's *Mrs Dalloway*. *The Trial*, an unfinished novel by Franz Kafka, who had died in 1924, was also published. Fortunately for posterity, Kafka's literary executor, Max Brod, decided to ignore the writer's request that these and other unpublished works should be destroyed. The architect Walter Gropius began his great Bauhaus buildings at Dessau, while in Paris, an Exhibition of Decorative Arts launched a style that could hardly have been more different in spirit from Surrealism – hard-edged, modernistic Art Deco.

Reichspräsident von Hindenburg nach der Eidesleistung, beim Abschreiten der Front vor dem Reichstagsgebäude am 12. 5. 25.

Bildarchiv Preussischer Kulturbesitz

President Hindenburg on duty

(left) On 12 May 1925, Field-Marshal von Hindenburg was formally sworn in as the new Reichspresident in the Reichstag building. His victory over the Russians at Tannenberg and the Masurian Lakes in 1914 had elevated him to the status of national hero and for the last year of the war he had been effectively in control of German civil and military policy. With defeat came revolution, the establishment of the Weimar Republic and the resultant tensions between the rightist old guard and the stirrings of leftist change. Hindenburg, already in his late seventies, had little influence on policy during his two terms as president; his acceptance of Hitler as Chancellor in 1933 spelt the end of the republic. Here the newly appointed Reichspresident inspects a military parade after leaving the Reichstag.

Nazi doctrine

(right) This cartoon satirizes contemporary lack of interest in Hitler's Mein Kampf *(My Struggle) published in two volumes in 1925 and 1926. Written during Hitler's 13 month spell of imprisonment after his abortive Munich 'Beer Hall Putsch' of 1923,* Mein Kampf *purports to be a political autobiography. In fact it is a clear expression of the Nazi leader's prejudiced assessment of the contemporary political scene together with his suggested extremist remedies. Hitler's doctrine of racial purity, his hatred of Jews and Communists, his advocacy of war and the German need to expand eastwards are all forcefully expressed in page after page of vehement prose. The world had been warned.*

John Goldblatt

BRIDGET RILEY

b.1931

Bridget Riley's work has won widespread international recognition and she is one of today's leading abstract painters. Born in London in 1931, she knew from childhood that she wished to be an artist. Her inspiration derives from her perception of and response to nature, colour and light, and she has a deep respect for the art of the past, especially that of Rubens, Seurat, Monet and Matisse – the great masters of colour.

After a series of highly original monochrome works, Bridget Riley moved on, in a deliberate, disciplined way, to explore the possibilities of colour. Her major works are characterized by large scale, a precise and meticulous finish, clarity of colour, and forms which allow long edges of colour to lie next to each other. This enables her to create works which give off the brilliant shimmer and subtle changes of light itself.

A Lifelong Dedication

From her earliest years Bridget Riley wanted to draw and paint, and her life has been devoted to her art. Constantly experimenting with new ideas, she retains a freshness of vision and openness of mind.

A Cornish childhood
Bridget Riley spent much of her childhood in a cottage near Padstow in Cornwall. During long walks taken along cliff tops and among the varied Cornish scenery, Bridget first became aware of the beauties of nature. The open skies and changing qualities of light were to affect profoundly her visual awareness.

Bridget Riley was born in South London on 24 April 1931. Her family is an unusual one and its members take pride in a tradition of independent behaviour and achievement. A distant ancestor is the great Liberal prime minister of the late 19th century, William Ewart Gladstone, but there are grandparents, great uncles and aunts who have made their own quiet mark on the world too.

Her parents set a high standard of family life, fostering close ties, affection and strength of character. Bridget has inherited much of her father's stoicism, inventiveness and optimism while her mother, as well as being optimistic was 'well read, unconventional, very much a product of the new world of the 1920s, and always willing to rethink attitudes to orthodox and accepted issues'. These are Bridget Riley's own words, but she is in many ways also describing herself.

Bridget's early formative and teenage years coincided with the Second World War and its austere aftermath. Her father was a prisoner of war and the years 1939-45 were spent with her mother, aunt and sister in Cornwall, in a cottage where life was spartan and simple. There was little in the way of formal schooling but life was fun and stimulating. There she learned to look at her surroundings with a freshness and acuteness of vision that is given to few people, and which was to become the basis of her visual life as a painter. Bridget was a willing and responsive child who knew from the beginning that she wanted to draw and paint, and who instinctively was able to see and marvel at the colours, patterns and vibrations produced by natural phenomena.

Her first experience of formal art training came at Cheltenham Ladies' College, which she attended

Portrait of her mother
(below) Bridget Riley's mother was an unconventional and open-minded woman who, with Bridget's aunt, helped to form her visual perception by pointing out the shapes and colour relationships of natural objects.

Derek Forss

Key Dates

1931 born in London

1939-45 spends childhood in Cornwall

1946-48 at Cheltenham Ladies' College

1949-52 attends Goldsmiths' College

1952-55 studies at Royal College of Art

1960 trip to Italy with Maurice de Sausmarez

1962 first solo show

1965 two major New York exhibitions

1968 wins International Painting Prize; formation of SPACE

1971 major European touring retrospective

1971-75 tours Europe

1981 trip to Egypt

1983 decorations for the Royal Liverpool Hospital; designs *Colour Moves*

The Bridge at Courbevoie/Courtauld Institute Galleries

Influence of Seurat
(above) Seurat's experiments with colour theory fascinated Bridget, and his pointillist technique was an important inspiration for her own development; in 1959, she made a copy of this work.

from age 15 to 17. She was released from the normal academic curriculum and allowed to work under the guidance of Colin Hayes, the school's art master, now a distinguished Royal Academician. Hayes introduced her to the work of great painters of the past, allowed her to attend life classes and furthered her interest in colour by showing her the example of Van Gogh.

From Cheltenham, Bridget went on to Goldsmiths' College in London. There she was encouraged by Sam Rabin, who furthered her understanding of drawing. He showed her Ingres' drawings, which are models of precise perception and clear, balanced execution, and they have remained a continuing inspiration.

A DIFFICULT PERIOD

There then followed a difficult and confusing three years at the Royal College of Art. Her contemporaries were a distinguished group including Peter Blake and John Bratby, but for Bridget the teaching and direction were unrewarding. She was reaching the point where she wanted to establish her own style and express herself in her own way which could not happen in an institutional framework. By sheer bad luck, on leaving the Royal College she had to devote her whole attention to nursing her father through a long illness following a car accident. She then became ill herself and was forced to convalesce and for three years she produced little or no work. However, two exhibitions in London, in 1956, helped to shape her creative thinking and sense of direction. The first was 'The Developing Process Exhibition' at the ICA, and the second was an exhibition of American Abstract Expressionist painters at the Tate Gallery, the first large exhibition of such works in England.

John Webb

Tonal landscape study, France
(left) This black pastel landscape was done during a journey through France in 1960 and shows Bridget's early interest in differing tonal contrasts.

Daily Mail 9th June 1965

OP ART

Op dress in a navy and white 'lightning' print by Veronica Marsh, 8i gns. Also available in navy on pale green and navy on turquoise.

Black crepe dress with a white zigzag across hip, by Simon Massey, 7 gns. Op shoes by Lotus, 89s.11d. The background is a white cotton carrier bag hand-printed with a black "bulls-eye" by Sally Jess. 70s.

Op beret and skirt in black and white sailcloth, beret 8gns., skirt 8gns., striped leather belt, 3gns. White skinny-rib sweater 29s. 11d. All by Paliandes.

PICTURES BY GORDON CARTER, DRAWING BY MAY ROUTH

Success and imitation
(above) 1965 witnessed international recognition for Bridget Riley in New York with two highly successful exhibitions. However, deep injustice followed when a dress firm used one of her paintings as a fabric design; she tried to sue, but under US law at that time there was no protection for the artist.

From 1959 onwards Bridget Riley's sense of purpose and creativity moved ahead with increasing confidence and speed. A trip to Italy the following year with Maurice de Sausmarez, director of Hornsey College of Art, produced many valuable experiences. Italian Renaissance art made a deep impression, notably Piero della Francesca's frescoes at Arezzo. The architecture, too, made its mark, especially the churches at Ravenna and the black and white Romanesque buildings at Pisa. Modern Italian art made a particular contribution through the work of the Futurists, who were displayed in a major exhibition at the Venice Biennale. Maurice de Sausmarez helped her to begin to understand modern art. With him she examined Italian Futurist work in detail and began her study of Seurat's use of colour. *Pink Landscape* (p.114) was painted as a result of this visit to Italy and shows both these influences.

In the autumn of 1960 Bridget Riley was back in England teaching at the Hornsey College of Art. There she began her first optical paintings and until 1966 all her work was based on a black and white monochrome palette. In these works she investigated many areas of perception; however this work, with its emphasis on optical effects, was never intended to be an end in itself.

The Impact of Egypt

A major breakthrough for Bridget Riley occurred after a visit to Egypt in 1981. She was forcibly struck by the palette used by the ancient Egyptian artists – a complete but basic palette of red, yellow, blue, turquoise and green. These five colours reflected the landscape of Egypt: desert, sky, sea, earth, water and vegetation, and were used by the Egyptians without alteration for their paintings, architecture, furniture, jewellery and pottery. On returning home, Bridget adopted this same basic palette, finding that she could use it to give her paintings a new breadth and intensity. The exciting discovery was that these colours retained their own individual brilliance, while interacting with each other to give a vibrant sense of light.

Tomb paintings
(left) Particularly striking to Bridget were the recently excavated tomb paintings of Luxor, where the colours of the Egyptian palette – still remarkably fresh – simply glowed with light.

Journey up the Nile
(right) Bridget and her friends spent three weeks travelling by train and car up the Nile valley from Cairo as far as Luxor, where time seemed to have stood still for thousands of years.

These were the years that laid the solid technical foundations for her painting. Her work was, and has always remained, instinctive. She is not dictated to by theory, but is guided by what she sees happening with her own eyes. She takes evident delight in showing that what happens and what can be seen to happen, can disprove and contradict established theories. The black and white paintings taught her a great deal about how perception functions both on a practical and aesthetic level and by 1966 she was able to leave monochrome and begin to broaden her palette, by introducing first grey, and then blue and red. Talking about this period, she quotes Monet – whom she much admires – as the artist who saw that too many colours are the enemy of colour. She explains her need to start with simple basic elements in order to have a firm foundation on which to build the complexity and richness which are a strong feature of her later work.

CRITICAL ACCLAIM

This period also witnessed Bridget's first critical recognition. From April to May 1962, her first solo show was held at Gallery One in London. In 1963 she won a prize at the important 'John Moore's Liverpool Exhibition' and the 'AICA Critics' Prize' in London. She won a Stuyvesant Foundation Bursary in 1964, and was represented in Exhibitions in London, and overseas in Europe, the USA and in Japan. In 1965 she attracted considerable notice at the 'Responsive Eye Exhibition' at the Museum of Modern Art in New York and one of her paintings was chosen as the illustration for the cover of the catalogue. Her first solo exhibition in the USA at the Richard Feigen Gallery was sold out on the first day – a remarkable achievement for an artist still in her early 30s.

A continual story of world-wide exhibitions, international recognition and honours has followed since. Notable among these are the

Camera Press

Hutchinson Library

Bridget with 'Continuum', 1963
(above) This photograph shows Bridget Riley at the entrance to her work, Continuum. *This coiled structure created such intense optical disturbances that to stand inside it caused a complete physical disorientation.*

'International Painting Prize' at the XXXIV Venice Biennale in 1968, a major retrospective exhibition which toured Europe in 1971 and a British Council touring exhibition to the United States, Australia and Japan in 1978-81. During this time, Bridget Riley was also working hard to create, with another artist, Peter Sedgley, the scheme known as SPACE (first mooted in 1968) to provide studios for young artists in the then derelict St Katherine's Dock in the Port of London.

These international exhibitions and recognition meant an opportunity to travel the world. Notable experiences whilst travelling in Europe were the discoveries of the Baroque churches of Southern Germany, the Tiepolo frescoes at Würzburg and

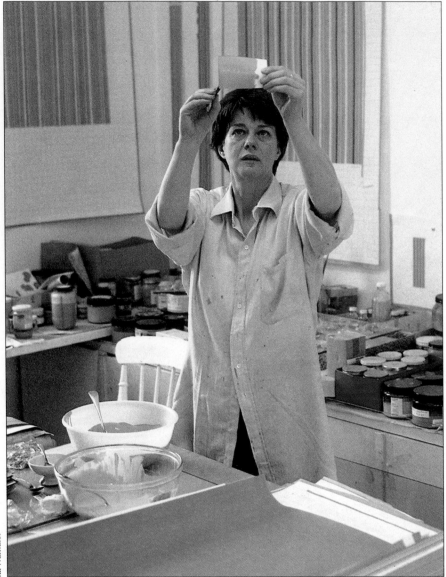

Bill Warhurst

train and car from Cairo up the Nile to Luxor and for three weeks they were steeped in the distant past and had no contact with any other works of art. This isolation was extremely beneficial for it had the effect of bringing ancient Egypt to life. What excited Bridget in particular was the discovery that the Egyptians had fixed a particular palette of five basic colours which they had used unchanged for 3000 years for all their art and artefacts. On the underground wall paintings of their burial chambers these five colours glowed with light and life as though the sun had been condensed in the rock tombs.

NEW INSPIRATION

On her return home, Bridget plunged with renewed enthusiasm into intense creative activity. Since beginning to work with colour in the late 1960s she had worked through several different groups of colours, each of which had proved to have limitations in that they never fully achieved the intensity and shimmer of light which she had always wanted to achieve. Ancient Egyptian civilisation inspired her to use a new group of

'Colour Moves'

In 1982-83 Bridget Riley was commissioned by Robert North, artistic director of the Ballet Rambert, to design the sets for a new ballet known as *Colour Moves*. The commission was an unusual one in that the designs for the sets preceded the composition of the music and the choreography, and actually provided the original inspiration for the work. In the ballet, which was first performed at the Edinburgh Festival in September 1983, there were five separate scenes with individual colour qualities, starting with grey and ending with a finale which gave a sense of the opening out of colour.

the paintings of Rubens in Munich. At the same time she established three studios: one in Cornwall, the place of her important childhood experiences; one in Holland Park in London, in a large spacious terrace house once occupied by her family; and one in the Vaucluse valley in Provence, which she visited for the first time in 1961 just as her painting was finding its direction and sense of purpose. These three locations, ranging from the peace of remote countryside to the bustle of the city and the international art world, each have their significance and mark important moments in her development and career.

Bridget Riley's paintings of the late 60s and 70s became principally concerned with the visual and emotional response to colour, and the palette and the forms were explored and varied. Something of a breakthrough in her work then occurred following a visit she made to Egypt in 1981. The journey was not undertaken with any particular expectation but Bridget found that the country cast a spell quite different from anywhere she had previously visited. She travelled with friends by

Mixing colours
(above) Bridget is shown here in her London studio mixing her current group of colours. The mixing stage is of vital importance because obtaining the correct hues, with absolutely the right tone and intensity, is essential to her works. Her canvases go through a great many preparatory stages before reaching completion – from small gouache studies, to the acrylic underpainting and finally, the oil finish.

Hospital decorations

(right) In 1983, Bridget was commissioned to design a decorative scheme for the Royal Liverpool Hospital. Her colourful murals, in horizontal strips of blues, yellow, pink and white, have transformed the grim interior.

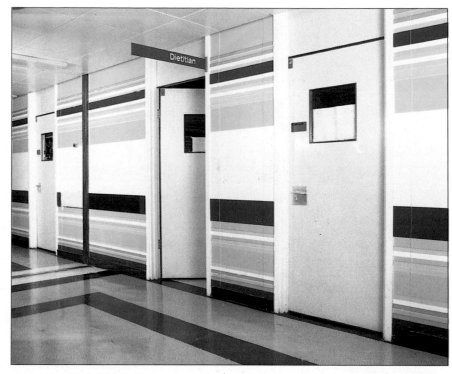

colours with which she was able to achieve this goal for the first time.

These new paintings have been the focus of Bridget Riley's creativity for most of the 1980s. There have been new honours, most notably her appointment as a Trustee of the National Gallery, London and two highly successful ventures into architecture and theatre design. In 1983 she was asked to advise on a scheme of decoration for the Royal Liverpool Hospital, a grim and anonymous modern building which created a bleak environment for its patients and whose corridors were regularly subjected to vandalism and graffiti. Bridget Riley's bands of optimistic colour transformed the building and the mood of its inhabitants and in addition removed the curse of vandalism. The same year she collaborated with the choreographer, Robert North, on a new ballet *Colour Moves* which was first performed at the Edinburgh Festival and then successfully toured.

It will be apparent from the above that Bridget Riley is an artist who surrounds herself with work and dedicates herself to it. She has consciously chosen not to take on the ties and obligations of family life but this does not mean she has cut herself off from the world. In her studios, and so in her life, there is an atmosphere of openness, inquisitiveness and a sense of purpose; and the seriousness which this purpose implies is balanced by a sense of fun. Conversation is easy for she is highly articulate and uses words and language with the same clarity and precision that she brings to her paintings. Bridget Riley, true to her family tradition, is unusual and remarkable both as a painter and as a person.

Colour vibrations

(right) This shows one of the five scenes from Colour Moves *with a dancer from the Ballet Rambert. The dancers were dressed as simple colours and their movement against the backcloth animated the static background, releasing colour vibrations and sensations to the audience.*

At work on a set

(left) Bridget is seen here with some of her assistants working on one of the sets for the ballet; in the background can be seen various small-scale models for the set. Bridget is quite used to working with other people and often collaborates with her assistants in the execution of her work.

Anthony Crickmay

Vaucluse valley, Provence

(below) One of Bridget's three studios is in the heart of Provence in southern France. She divides her time between this and her studios in London and Cornwall.

Explorer/F. Jalain

Sight and Colour

Bridget Riley's work is inspired by the excitement and pleasure she gains from what she sees, and by a remarkable sensitivity to colour and a fascination with its 'activity'.

Juda Rowan

themselves which constituted the essence of vision, but that they were agents of a greater reality, of the bridge which sight throws from our innermost heart to the furthest extension of that which surrounds us.' The complement to this inspiration is the desire to build and organize, and so bring into existence a new entity which will in turn precipitate some fresh way of seeing again something that has been experienced but forgotten with the passage of time.

Bridget Riley works with simple elements so that her work can have the maximum clarity and purity. From the early 1960s, these elements were basic to the point where she used only monochrome, black and white forms such as the

Bridget Riley is an artist who works slowly and very methodically, continually making fresh discoveries and building on them as she goes along. She derives excitement and inspiration from many sources – from paintings, from nature, from architecture, from people – and she is moved to express something that is also felt as an emotion.

The basis of her visual life was formed during her childhood in Cornwall and she still draws on her memories of her first visual discoveries among the sunlight, the water and wild countryside. 'The pleasures of sight take you by surprise. They are sudden, swift and unexpected,' she has written. 'They are essentially enigmatic and elusive . . . momentarily turning the commonplace into the ravishing. Naturally as a child one is more open to such experiences . . . It seems to me that as an artist one's work lies here. I realized partially through my own experience and partially through the great masters of Modern Art that it was not the actual sea, the individual rocks or valleys in

Pink Landscape (1960)
(above) In this hot Italian landscape, form almost disappears in the glitter of heat-haze and reflected light. The tiny coloured dots are derived from Seurat's pointillist technique, but are large enough to impinge as forms in their own right.

Hidden Squares (1961)
(right) As in Pink Landscape, *the forms are hidden. The diameter of the circle is the same as the side of the square, so perception is confused, losing the forms and finding them again.*

Juda Rowan

Where (1964)
(left) Here the structure of gradually compressing circles is constant, but the tonal sequences change at different rates. This sets up vertical forces which carry the eye out only to be drawn in again by the inward movement.

Cataract 3 (1967)
(detail below) Two opposed colours are used to form an exhilarating visual torrent, in which the extreme angle creates bands of compression which shoot across the potentially placid curves like bolts of energy.

British Council Collection

triangle, curve, oval and zigzag. The forms were varied and the paintings developed so that they presented dematerialized vibrating sensations of space. She then began to introduce colour, first by way of greys, then tinted greys, and then pure colour. As colour was introduced, Bridget stabilized the forms and made them constant, so that it was colour, not forms, that became the variable factor. Recently she has used the plain stripe since it is less intrusive than the curve, and is a form which produces long edges with comparatively little body. It is along these edges of juxtaposed colour that her works generate their own brilliance and vibration and stimulus to sight.

METHODICAL PROGRESS

Bridget Riley's major works are large scale and may take six to nine months to develop. The artist begins by making small colour studies in gouache to investigate the activity and reaction of colours. All paints are hand mixed by Bridget since the exact hue and intensity is vital, and must be kept constant. Some of these studies prove successful and others fail entirely, but together they lead to a full size paper and gouache cartoon which prefigures the final work. When the cartoon is finally judged to be successful, a large canvas is carefully prepared. This is ruled up, underpainted in acrylic colours, and overpainted in oils. All the painting is done by hand, with the help of assistants, to give the greatest crispness to the long edges: masking tape is never used.

Absolute precision and a meticulously accurate finish are essential to Bridget Riley's work, since variations in colour or texture would set up a destructive interference with the purity of the colour, and distract from the perception of that undefinable luminosity pervading the work.

When a painting is completed, it is given its title. The title reflects the sensation emanating from the work and may refer to qualities of light, the seasons, different lands or cultural artefacts.

The full visual effect of Bridget Riley's work can only really be experienced in front of the painting itself, and even then the viewer needs to experiment and move around to find the points at which the elusive colour sensations are released.

Since starting to use colour, Bridget has worked with a great number of different groups of

carefully selected limited colours. All the groups have been judged by a double standard: there is the existence of the actual colours, and there are the other colours and light sensations which are generated by the juxtaposition of the long narrow stripes or curves. Frequently the artist has found she has had to sacrifice the beauty of the painted colour in order to preserve and enhance the faint and fleeting glimmers they generate. The significance of the palette adopted after Bridget's visit to Egypt in 1981 is that this was a group of colours which worked together as a group, retained their individual brilliance, and still

Deny I (1966)
(right) This painting is closely related to Static I *(p.122), but is cast into a sombre and mysterious key by the use of tone and colour. Set on a cool grey, the tilting warm grey ovals gradate towards the tone of the ground, forming a shadowy 'V'.*

COMPARISONS

Abstract Art

Abstract art first appeared in Europe as early as 1910. Mondrian was one of the first European abstract painters whose best-known works are characterized by a delicate balance of the horizontal and vertical and the three primary colours. In his late paintings, the tranquillity of earlier work is disrupted in favour of new forms and colours, and the visual beat and dazzle they produce is not unlike that found in some of Bridget Riley's paintings. Jackson Pollock's large canvases, with their thick flowing paint apparently randomly applied, are at first sight far removed from Bridget's carefully controlled work, but they share an openness and sense of movement and rhythm.

Jackson Pollock (1912-56) **Convergence** (1952)
(below) A pioneer of abstract painting in America, Jackson Pollock developed his abstract style – known as Action Painting – during the 1940s. His canvases were created by a controlled pouring of paint across their surface to give a vibrant texture and then carefully cut up to form the final works.

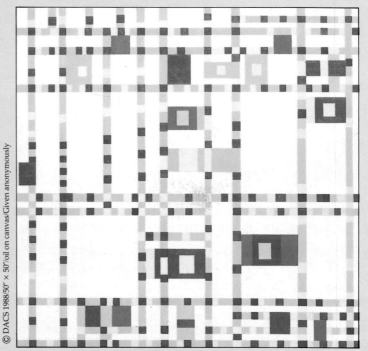

Collection, The Museum of Modern Art, New York

Piet Mondrian (1872-1944) **Broadway Boogie Woogie**
(above) A Dutch painter, Mondrian refined his abstraction to express 'dynamic movement in equilibrium'. One of his last and greatest achievements, this work is a controlled explosion of colour, inspired by jazz and Mondrian's American experience.

Albright Knox Art Gallery, Buffalo, New York

Juda Rowan

generated new colours and light effects. 'It was as though a veil had been lifted', she has said.

It is not possible to say or even predict the last word on Bridget Riley's work, since by its very nature it is not the sort of painting that will fall into easy repetition or be content with a popular image or single theme, and she is always experimenting with new ideas which mark new departures. She creates work which is demanding both of herself and the spectator. No painting is a repetition or even a variation of another, for each is created afresh, springing from fresh observations, perceptions and experiences, and asking for a correspondingly new participation and vision from those who go to meet them.

TRADEMARKS

The Band

The repeating band is the most important formal device in Bridget Riley's work. It may be straight or curved, vertical or horizontal. In a black and white painting like *Fall* (detail right) it carries the contrast and the rhythm. In later work it is a way of putting colours close together so that they interact.

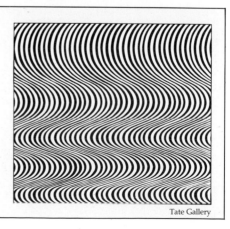

Tate Gallery

THE MAKING OF A MASTERPIECE

Paean

With its monumental verticality and brilliant pure colour, *Paean* looks as though it should belong with the Egyptian paintings of the 1980s. In fact it was painted seven years earlier, in 1973, before the colour-curve paintings like *Rill* (pp.126-7) and *Entice 2*. Made up of bands of colour which vary in colour-character, the whole surface of the painting has a vibrating, breathing quality, each band seeming to advance and recede in turn as the eye scans across. Over nine and a half feet tall, *Paean* is Bridget Riley's largest painting to date. The towering verticals accumulate power by their very length, and the repeated rhythm, modulated by colour, gives the surface an almost architectural quality.

> 'The music of colour, that's what I want.'
> Bridget Riley

Colour studies

(below) These six colour studies help to reveal the structure of the finished painting. Colour is limited to red, blue and green, and organized into bands of three stripes, with one colour 'surrounding' another. Each band takes on a character of its own, depending on the colours used.

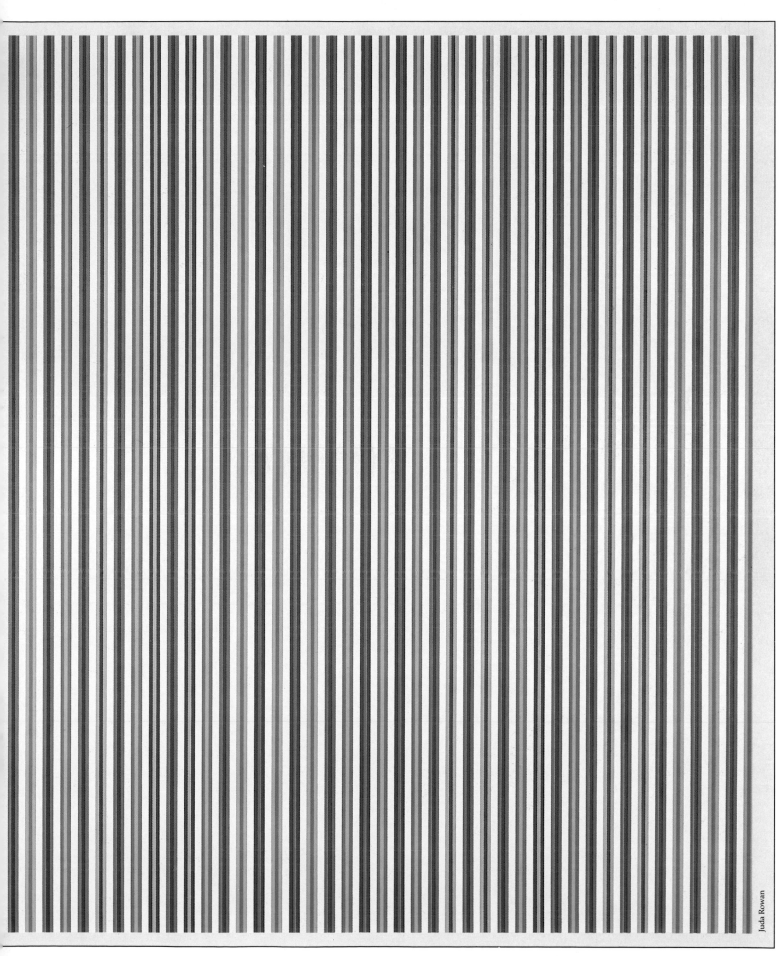

Gallery

In black and white paintings like Blaze I and Shiver, Bridget Riley explored basic visual issues, such as the production of luminosity by contrast and the creation of space by implied movement, with great precision. An important legacy of this period was the use of curved or straight bands. These proved the perfect vehicle for colour and became a

Juda Rowan

Blaze I *1962*
43″ × 43″ Private Collection, London

In this dramatic image the zig-zag lines are stretched and compressed at different points, owing to the changing relationship of the circles to one another. As we look, the energies thus created seem to explode into fierce, juddering movements which chase each other round, while a burst or 'blaze' of light permeates the painting from the centre.

cornerstone of future work. At first, colour was often used in series resembling earlier tonal gradations, but this soon gave way to pure colours that remained constant throughout a work. In paintings like Rill, Bridget Riley's use of colour curves to create a seamless envelope of luminosity reached a peak of refinement.

One characteristic of the curve was that it would not easily carry full, strong colour. In the 'Egyptian' series of the early 1980s, a small number of intense colours were grouped into free organizations of straight vertical bands. This led on to the visual splendour of paintings like Rose Return, where rich colour becomes the whole subject.

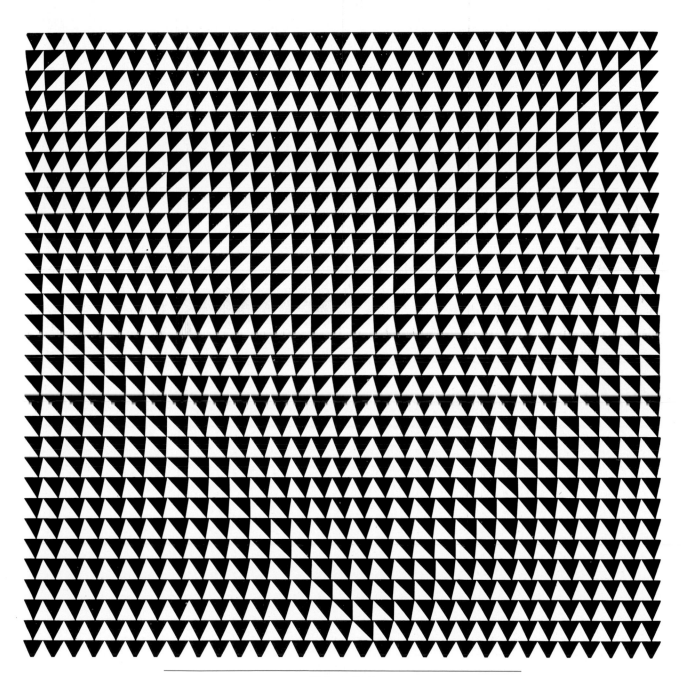

Juda Rowan

Shiver *1964*
27″ × 27″ Tony Curtis, Los Angeles

*The point of a triangle moves, in sequence, backwards and forwards
along a horizontal line. The whole field becomes uncertain, wavering,
about to collapse, as the diagonal stability on which the square is
based is called into question. Across the surface run mysterious
shadows and movements, like wind across a lake.*

121

Juda Rowan

Static 1 *1966*
90″ × 90″ Hannelore B. Schulhof, New York

Tiny ovals, turning in sequence, are distributed across the surface. As the eye travels over them they become activated, spinning and wriggling in their places until bursts of energy are discharged throughout the painting. These bursts, together with the opening and closing intervals between the elements, create a curving space.

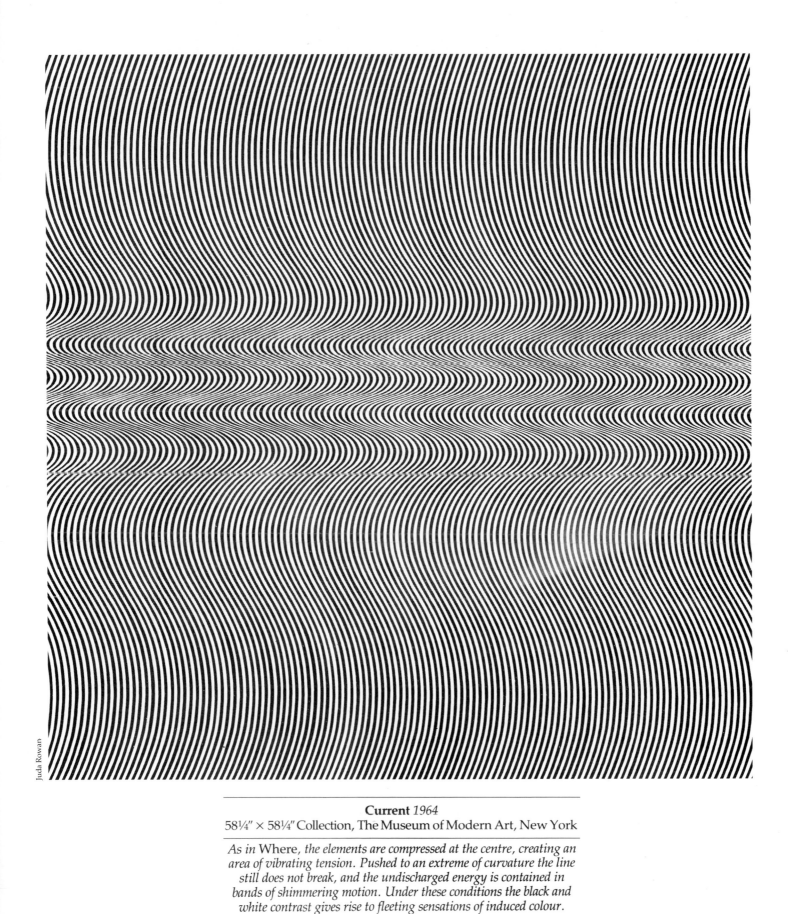

Juda Rowan

Current *1964*
58¼″ × 58¼″ Collection, The Museum of Modern Art, New York

As in Where, *the elements are compressed at the centre, creating an area of vibrating tension. Pushed to an extreme of curvature the line still does not break, and the undischarged energy is contained in bands of shimmering motion. Under these conditions the black and white contrast gives rise to fleeting sensations of induced colour.*

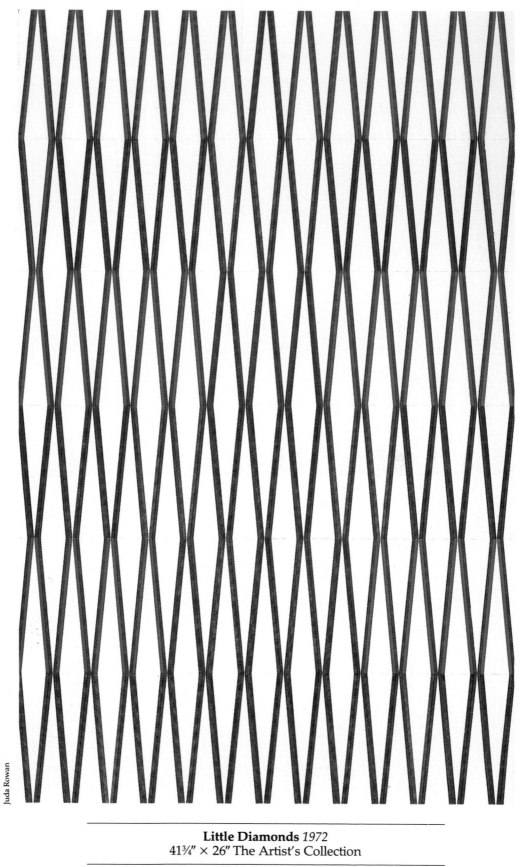

Juda Rowan

Little Diamonds *1972*
41¾″ × 26″ The Artist's Collection

*The effect of colour-spread into the white is here caught and
concentrated as if in a net, with particularly intense colour-spreading
occurring at the points. The red produces a constant warm glow, while
two alternating colour gradations, from green to turquoise and from
turquoise to blue, create bands of cold luminosity across the canvas.*

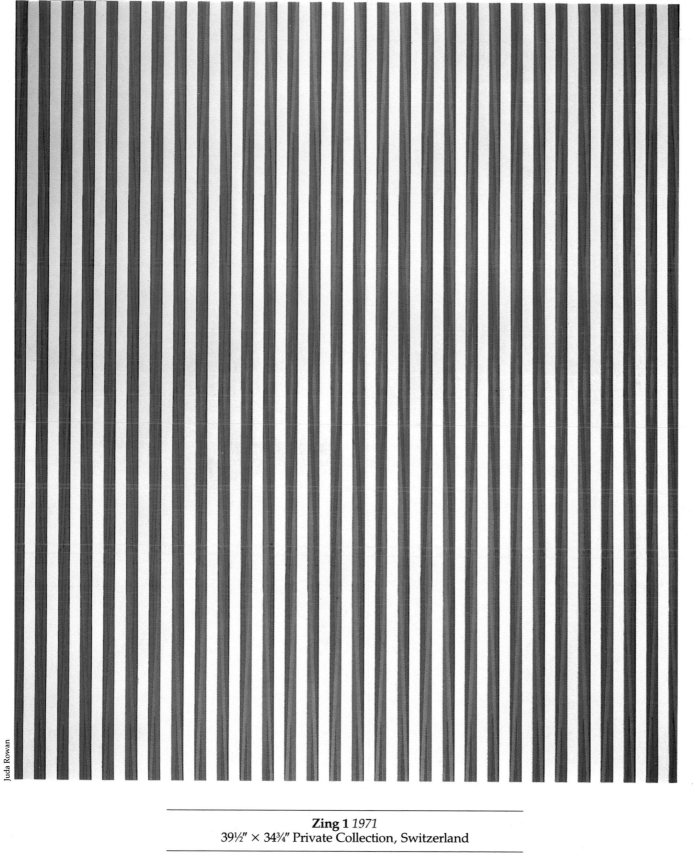

Juda Rowan

Zing 1 *1971*
39½″ × 34¾″ Private Collection, Switzerland

Glowing bands of colour appear to span the painting as the red, blue and green cross over one another, influencing the white ground. The colours themselves react together so, for instance, the red appears orange when next to the green and violet next to the blue. In this way a complex set of relationships emerges.

Juda Rowan

Rill *1976*
89¾″ × 37″ Private
Collection, Cincinnatti

*Here twisted skeins of
colour are woven into an
unbroken 'colour envelope'
by means of the cross-over
principle used in Zing 1
(p.125). Structure is now
purely a vehicle for colour
and even seems to
disappear, as the light grey
of the ground accepts colour
'influence and 'fills in'
across the surface.*

Streak 2 *1979*
44¾″ × 99″ Thyssen Bornesmisza Collection

*A sensation of speed, unease, even of danger arises as the field is penetrated
by an opposing current that disrupts the calm, wave-like rhythm. At the
edges of this dividing movement, where the normal relationship of the
curves is altered, an extra charge of colour is released. This is echoed by
colour flashes in the rest of the painting, which seem to 'streak' along, as
though they are given an extra impetus by the tripping-up of the beat.*

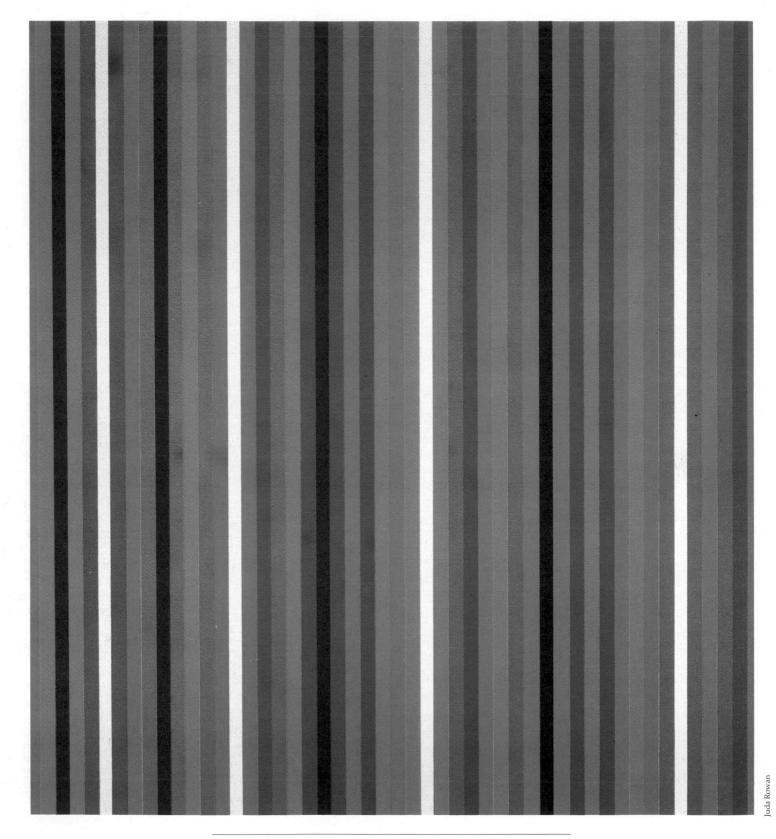

Juda Rowan

Gather *1980*
34″ × 30¾″ Private Collection, New York

The earliest 'Egyptian' paintings mark the beginnings of free colour organization. Here there are several older ideas, such as the overall blue ground and the rhythm increasing regularly towards an edge. But these appear in a much freer context in which colours seem to step forwards or backwards to make a real colour-space.

Juda Rowan

Rose Return *1985*
67¾″ × 56¼″ Juda Rowan Gallery, London

The organization is wholly free and visually determined, without regular sequence. Here the idea of a coloured ground has been replaced by an overall colour sensation to which all the colour groupings contribute while retaining their own identity. These groups create a steady, though not regular, rhythm of advancing and receding space.

The Swinging Sixties

England in the 60s was overflowing with creative energy – energy that expressed itself, for the most part, not in 'adult' art forms, but in 'swinging' young fashion and pop culture.

The Wilson years
(below) Following the general election of 1964, the Labour party formed a government under Harold Wilson. As prime minister, Wilson carefully cultivated a popular 'ordinary bloke' image, and was a frequent a target of the satirical magazine Private Eye.

In 1966, Roger Miller topped the record charts with a song which contained the line, 'England swings like a pendulum do' The song was partly tongue-in-cheek – and considered less than 'cool' by the 'in crowd' – but the phrase captures perfectly the heady mixture of pride and optimism that infected England between 1963 and 1967.

Summer of 1963 had seen the country rocked by the scandal of Cabinet Minister John Profumo's affair with a 19-year-old call girl called Christine Keeler, who was also involved with the naval attaché at the Soviet embassy. But for the young

'England swings'
(right) In the 60s, England set the trends for the rest of the world to follow, and the Union Jack became a symbol of youthful pride and optimism. The country's 'swinging' image was reflected in its innovative fashions – of which the miniskirt, designed by Mary Quant, was the most sensational example.

PRIVATE EYE

We can't go on meeting like this

THE QUEEN AND MR WILSON THE TRUTH

Popperfoto

swingers, the public indignation was just the death throes of an outdated 'square' morality. From now on, society would be more tolerant, and attitudes towards morals and sex more liberal (or 'permissive' as critics carped).

When a Labour Government was elected in 1964 on a paper-thin majority, after more than 13 years of Tory rule, the revolution in attitudes seemed well under way. The new Prime Minister, Harold Wilson, who was immensely popular with the young, predicted a bright future, forged in 'the white heat of technological revolution'.

London, especially, announced itself as a colourful, exciting, modern and, above all, youthful city – the city that set the trends for the rest of the world to follow. In a famous article in *Time* magazine of 16 April 1966, Martin Lasky coined the epithet 'Swinging London' and painted a picture of a city brimming with vitality and talent.

In those years, the trend-setters in London developed an image that made it seem the most exciting city in the world – and made outsiders long to be part of the 'in crowd'. In image at least, the lifestyle of these swingers was sexually promiscuous – every young girl was supposed to be on the new Pill. It was hedonistic, too, with the emphasis very much on fun. When they were not strolling down Carnaby Street or the King's Road discovering the latest fashion, they were partying in Chelsea, carousing in the fashionable San Lorenzo restaurant in Kensington, or dancing the night away in one of the new discotheques.

YOUNG CHIC

There had been nightclubs in London before, but the new discotheques, such as the Ad-Lib in Leicester Square (open February 1964) and the Scotch of St James, seemed to symbolize the modern lifestyle. In a contemporary report, George Melly described the Ad-Lib as 'dedicated to the triumph of style. It may be chic, non-committed and amoral, but it's also cool, tolerant and physically beautiful. It's essentially to do with being young . . .'

The discotheques, it was claimed, were the epitome of the new classless society. Anyone who had the talent or the looks could become part of the 'in crowd' – as the success of young men such as photographer David Bailey, artist David Hockney, actor Albert Finney and, above all, numerous pop musicians seemed to bear witness.

All over the country, young swingers followed the movements of their heroes in London avidly, picking up on the latest fashion, the trendiest pop music and the current buzz words. Millions of teenagers tuned in every Friday night to the television pop music show *Ready, Steady, Go!* or listened to the continuous output of pop music broadcast from ships in the North Sea by the illegal 'pirate' radio stations, Radio Caroline and Radio London – until they were outlawed in 1967.

The real explosion of young talent was in pop music and fashion. All over the country, young

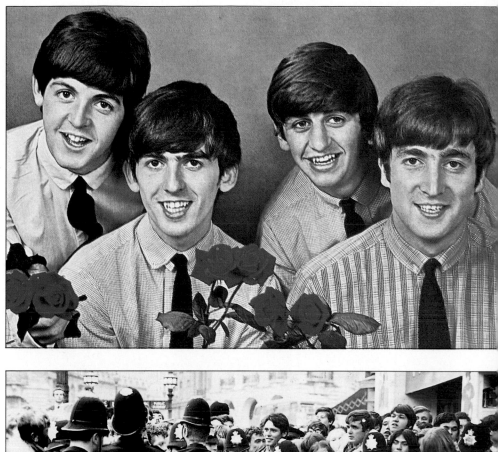

Rex Features

Rex Features

boys at school or at work saved up a few pounds to buy guitars and drums, and soon thousands of garages and bedrooms began to reverberate to the rhythm of embryo pop groups. Some of these groups got to play in the new clubs, such as London's Marquee and 100 Club. A few, very few, made a record and achieved stardom.

Of those that made it, none had quite the same impact as the most famous group of all, the Beatles. At the end of 1962, they were still playing to small audiences in Liverpool's Cavern Club. A year later, they had an unbroken string of No. 1 hits to their name, and whenever they appeared in public, they were greeted by thousands of screaming fans – a phenomenon soon christened by the press as 'Beatlemania'.

No other group could match the Beatles'

The 'Fab Four'
(above) In January 1963, the Beatles hit the top of the charts with Please, Please Me, *the first of a string of No. 1 records. Nine months later, their appearance on the live TV show, 'Sunday Night at the London Palladium', ensured them overnight fame. The hysterical behaviour of their fans hit the headlines, too – a phenomenon that was soon christened 'Beatlemania'.*

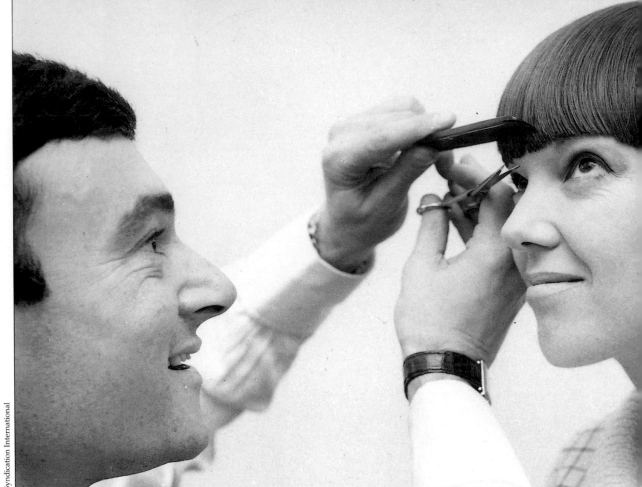

Quant and Sassoon
(right) Fashion designer Mary Quant wanted 'young people to have a fashion of their own, absolutely 20th-century fashion'. The finishing touch to her 'total look' – which included matching handbags and make-up – was provided by hairdresser, Vidal Sassoon. His hair creations were so successful that by 1965 he had opened a salon on New York's Madison Avenue.

Twiggy
(below) Twiggy, a 17-year-old Cockney model, was the ideal shape of the 60s' girl: slender, flat-chested, with long legs, and weighing only six and a half stone.

success, but the Rolling Stones, whose wild image outraged 'squares' and delighted 'swingers', had an enormous following. And every week, the clubs of London sang the praises of a new group – such as the Small Faces, the Kinks and the Who.

For members of the London scene, it was essential to wear the right clothes, for fashion had undergone a revolution. Previously, young people had tended to dress like their parents; now they had exciting clothes designed exclusively for them and special shops in which to buy them.

The idea of young fashion had begun with the designs of Mary Quant in the 1950s, but it was only in the mid-60s that it really caught on. By 1965, there were 'boutiques' (following Mary Quant's 'Bazaar') all along London's King's Road and in several towns and cities. Much to the astonishment of older people, young girls began to wear mini-skirts, barely a few inches long – as if to emphasize that these clothes were exclusively for the young. The need to market the latest 'look' made stars of talented fashion photographers such as David Bailey and Terence Donovan and top models such as Jean Shrimpton and Twiggy. And the stylish modern haircuts that featured in these looks made a household name of a young hairdresser called Vidal Sassoon.

MOD FASHIONS

Meanwhile, London's Carnaby Street was becoming a mecca for all 'dedicated (male) followers of fashion'. John Stephens had started the ball rolling here in the late 50s with his boutique catering for the rather dandy young modernists or 'mods'. Other clothes shops soon followed and, by 1963, Carnaby Street was a compulsory stopping-off point for young mods in town to visit Soho music clubs like the Scene. The mid-60s saw an unusual flowering of young talent in more conventional fields, too. There was a group of innovative artists, some of them already famous such as the Pop Artists Richard Hamilton and R. B. Kitaj, some of them just beginning to make a name

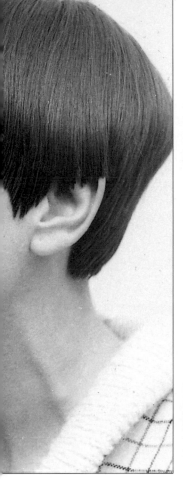

Carnaby Street
(*left*) *In the 1950s, rents in Carnaby Street were the cheapest in central London, encouraging young boutique owners, like John Stephens, to move in. By the early 60s, the street was a mecca for mods and pop-stars, who travelled there on their scooters or in their Austin Minis, the car which fast became the most popular of the 60s.*

The Flower Children
(*below*) *Towards the end of the 60s, a new fashion emerged, influenced by the new drug culture of hallucinatory LSD and marijuana. The flower people, or 'hippies', were essentially an American invention – middle-class pacifists who were dedicated to creating an alternative society, based on a 'return to nature' and sustained by music.*

for themselves, such as the sculptress Elizabeth Frink and the painter Bridget Riley. But it was the success of David Hockney – young, articulate and working-class – at the end of the 60s, that seemed most indicative of the mood of the times.

There was innovation in the theatre, too, with 1964 seeing such theatrical milestones as Peter Brook's brilliant production of the chilling *Marat/ Sade*, and Joe Orton's outrageous *Entertaining Mr Sloane*. Experimental theatre was breaking down the traditional barriers between actors and audience and, in 1964, there were the bizarre 'Happenings' in which anything might happen – from semi-naked women gliding through the audience in wheelbarrows to the removal of the entire contents of a house around invited guests watching a film unawares.

The fashion for satire seemed especially subversive. It began in 1960 in the theatre with a group of college graduates, including Jonathan Miller and Alan Bennet, in a revue called *Beyond The Fringe*, and moved on to television in 1961 with the notorious *That Was The Week That Was*. TW3 (as it came known) so regularly ridiculed public figures that the Postmaster-General, Reginald Bevins, resolved to 'do something about it' – only a note from Prime Minister Harold Macmillan saying simply, 'Oh no you won't!' stayed his hand. John Wells, who appeared in revues in Soho's Establishment Club, wrote, 'We really began to believe that we were in some sense underminers and detonators of politicians . . . that it was thanks to us Macmillan had collapsed.'

Wells' and his fellow satirists' belief in their power to change the world is typical of the optimism of the era – typical of the faith in the

future that gave many young people the will to try out ideas and realize their talents. Jean Shrimpton, the leading fashion model of the day later commented, 'There was energy then, and if you had an idea, however silly, you could get it on the road. People were willing to listen – too much so, but it was better than not listening at all . . . It was a terribly naive period . . . it was like falling in love.'

135

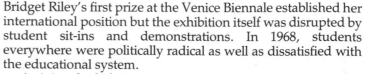

A Year in the Life 1968

In the year that Bridget Riley established her international reputation, student unrest spread across the western world and America was shocked by two political assassinations. A civil rights movement sprang up in Northern Ireland, while in Czechoslovakia, dissent was suppressed by Soviet tanks.

Bridget Riley's first prize at the Venice Biennale established her international position but the exhibition itself was disrupted by student sit-ins and demonstrations. In 1968, students everywhere were politically radical as well as dissatisfied with the educational system.

Activists had their greatest impact in France, where the '22nd of March' movement began at the University of Nanterre under the leadership of sociology student, Daniel Cohn-Bendit. On Friday, May 3, the student revolt took off in Paris. Peaceful demonstrations were quickly turned into mass insurrection as police moved in with tear gas and clubs. A week later the barricades were up in the Latin Quarter where savage battles between students and police took place. Reversing the official trend of repression, President de Gaulle conceded some of the

Popperfoto

Soviet dissident

(above) In 1968 Alexander Solzhenitsyn published two powerful novels, both outside the Soviet Union. Based on his experience of stomach cancer while imprisoned in a labour camp, Cancer Ward *explores the attitudes to life of a group of hospitalized Russians faced with imminent death from cancer;* The First Circle *is set in a scientific research station run by the secret police. Solzhenitsyn also completed* The Gulag Archipelago *during this year, a book which was to lead to his ejection from Soviet Russia in 1974.*

The Apollo 8 launch

(right) The Apollo programme was initiated in 1962 by President John F. Kennedy with the express aim of a manned moon landing before 1970. 1968 witnessed three Apollo launches, the last being that of Apollo 8, the first manned spacecraft to orbit the moon. The historic manned moon landing was to occur in July 1969, well before schedule.

Popperfoto

students' demands and emerged apparently unscathed, winning a significant election victory and then sacking his too-popular prime minister, Georges Pompidou. The shooting of the student leader, Rudi Dutschke, sparked off riots in West Berlin, while in America, Columbia University was paralysed by a student occupation, exacerbated by unnecessarily heavy-handed police action.

ANTI-WAR PROTESTS

One aspect of student politics was opposition to US military intervention in Vietnam. In January 1968, the communists' Tet offensive showed that, despite intensive US bombing of North Vietnam, they were capable of seizing a major town – Hue, and of even penetrating the presidential palace and the US Embassy compound in the capital, Saigon. Anti-war protests now redoubled, and the US will to win began to flag. As peace talks with the communists got under way, US bombing of North Vietnam was partially, then completely, suspended. But the political scene was also influenced by two assassinations. In April, the black civil rights leader, Martin Luther King, was shot in Memphis; and two months later, Senator Robert Kennedy was shot in his Los Angeles hotel at the beginning of his campaign to win the Democratic nomination. In the November presidential election, the Republican, Richard Nixon made a remarkable political come-back to defeat Hubert Humphrey, the Democratic candidate. Nixon had taken a strong stand on the 'law and order' issue. His victory signalled a move to the Right in American politics.

Student revolt
(right) The student riots in Paris during May and June 1968 began with no more than a protest meeting at the Sorbonne calling for the relaxation of restrictions mixed with left-wing opposition to the war in Vietnam. It was the brutal tactics of the police that turned the affair into a succession of bloody battles, mostly fought on the streets of the Latin Quarter. Here riot police equipped with batons and shields attempt to charge demonstrators on the Boulevard St Germain.

Topham Picture Library

The assassination of Robert Kennedy
(left) At 12.17 pm on 5 June 1968, Robert Kennedy, brother of the assassinated American President, John F. Kennedy, was shaking hands with kitchen staff at the Ambassador Hotel in Los Angeles. He was in relaxed but determined mood, being about to celebrate his winning the Democratic presidential nomination for California. There was a burst of gunfire and Kennedy fell, shot through the head. Although he was rushed to hospital and had emergency treatment, he died 25 hours later. His assassin, Sirhan Sirhan, a Jordanian illegal immigrant, was discovered to have had no political motive for the murder.

Bill Eppridge & Don Dorman/Life/© Time Inc 1968/Colorific

137

In January, Alexander Dubček became leader of communist Czechoslovakia and began to sweep away relics of the Stalinist past. But the USSR found the changes disquieting, and on the night of 20-21 August, Warsaw Pact tanks entered Czechoslovakia. Dubček's experiment in 'socialism with a human face' was over.

Other notable events of the year included the first successful heart transplant by Dr Christiaan Barnard, the election of Pierre Trudeau as Canadian Prime Minister, and the North Korean seizure of the US naval intelligence ship, *Pueblo*, (for alleged trespass in Korean waters) and extortion of an apology from the USA. Jacqueline Kennedy married Aristotle Onassis; and at the Mexico Olympics, two black US medallists created a sensation by raising their fists in Black Power salutes. A peaceful civil rights movement emerged among Northern Ireland's Catholics aimed at ending anti-Catholic discrimination. But clashes with the largely Protestant police and with followers of Ian Paisley, provided warnings that protests might not always remain peaceful. Race relations in Britain deteriorated alarmingly and British approaches to join the EEC continued to be rebuffed.

Landmarks in the field of entertainment during this year included the liberation of British theatre from 250 years of censorship; the Beatles remained highly creative, recording *Lady Madonna* and *Hey Jude*, founding their own firm, Apple, and appearing as cartoon characters in the film, *Yellow Submarine*. Gore Vidal published his trans-sexual comedy, *Myra Breckinridge* and Stanley Kubrick's classic futurist film, *2001: A Space Odyssey* was released.

Russian tanks on the streets of Prague

(right) In January 1968, Alexander Dubček took on the post of Czechoslovak Party Secretary against a background of rising liberalism. His promise to 'remove everything that strangles scientific and artistic creativity' was not appreciated by Moscow. In August, Soviet bloc armed forces invaded the country.

Topham Picture Library

Papal infallibility?

(left) On 29 July 1968 Pope Paul VI delivered the papal pronouncement Humanae Vitae *confirming the church's traditional condemnation of birth control. It was a surprising decision in view of the more liberal attitudes of the Second Vatican Council (1962-3) and the majority decision of a papal panel of experts in favour of change.*

Popperfoto

GALLERY GUIDE

Kandinsky

Kandinsky's work is well distributed in European collections. The strongest individual holding is at the Städtische Galerie, Munich, which includes pictures from the Gabriele Münter Foundation. Not surprisingly, this gallery is particularly rich in paintings from Kandinsky's early career and from his association with *Der Blaue Reiter*. Important works from this period can also be found at the Kunstsammlung Nordrhein-Westfalen, Düsseldorf, at the Stedelijk Museum, Amsterdam (*Houses at Murnau* and *The Orient*), and at the Musée d'Art Moderne in Paris. Kandinsky's Bauhaus phase is well-represented at the Boymans van Beuningen Museum, Rotterdam, which contains such splendid paintings as *Keeping Quiet* (1924) and *Whimsical* (1930). In America, the most extensive collection is at the Solomon R. Guggenheim Museum, New York, although the Museum of Modern Art, New York, and the Busch-Reisinger Museum at Harvard University also own samples of the artist's work.

Malevich

In the West, the finest collection of the artist's paintings is to be found in the Stedelijk Museum, Amsterdam. This consists of works brought over for Malevich's Berlin exhibition of 1927, which were entrusted to the architect, Hugo Häring, after the painter's premature recall to Russia, and which eventually passed to the Stedelijk. The collection is particularly strong in examples of his Neo-Primitive and Suprematist styles. In America, there is a fine general collection in the Museum of Modern Art, New York, while at Yale University, there is the most remarkable of Malevich's Cubo-Futurist works, *The Knife-Grinder* (p.57). In Russia,

his work is best seen at the Tretyakov Gallery, Moscow, and in the State Museum, Leningrad.

Miró

The vast majority of Miró's paintings are in the United States, many of them still in private hands. The most extensive single collection is at the Museum of Modern Art, New York, which covers all aspects of his work. Other examples can be found in Buffalo, Philadelphia and at the Art Institute of Chicago, which owns a rare example of his portraiture. In addition, both the Wadsworth Athenaeum, Hartford, Connecticut, and Washington University, St Louis, Missouri own notable variants of Miró's biomorphic 'Compositions'. The artist also executed large-scale murals and these can be found in the Hilton Hotel, Cincinnati, the Graduate Center at Harvard University, and, in Paris, at Unesco.

Riley

A very high proportion of Riley's work is in private hands. In public collections, the most representative selection is to be found at the Tate Gallery, London. This includes several versions of *Nineteen Greys*, along with examples of her vertical line compositions (*Late Morning*, 1968, and *Achaian*, 1981) and one of the 'wave' paintings (*To a Summer's Day*). Elsewhere in Britain, the Ferens Art Gallery, in Kingston-upon-Hull, owns the disorientating *Around*, while the Ulster Museum, Belfast, houses *Cataract IV*. In the USA, samples of Riley's 'wave' pictures can be seen in the Cleveland Museum of Art (drawing for *Elapse*) and in the Albright-Knox Art Gallery (*Drift No. 2*), while the Art Institute of Chicago possesses the remarkable *Ascending and Descending Hero* (1965).

BIBLIOGRAPHY

S. Alexandrian, *Surrealist Art*, Thames and Hudson, New York, 1985
A. Bovi, *Kandinsky*, Hamlyn, London, 1971
C. Gray, *The Russian Experiment in Art 1863-1922*, Thames and Hudson, New York, 1986
W. Haftman, *Painting in the Twentieth Century*, Holt, Rinehart & Winston, New York, 1965
M. Lacoste, *Kandinsky*, Crown, New York, 1979
R. Penrose, *Miró*, Thames and Hudson, New York, 1985
H. Roethel, *Kandinsky*, Hudson Hills, New York, 1979

J. Rothenstein, *Modern English Painters, Vol III: Wood to Hockney*, St Martin's, New York, 1974
M. de Sausmarez, *Bridget Riley*, Studio Vista, London, 1970
W. Schmalenbach, *Picasso to Lichtenstein*, Salem House, New York, 1985
D. Thompson (intro), *Bridget Riley*, Exhibition Catalogue, Sidney Janis Gallery, New York, 1975
P. Vergo (intro), *Abstraction: Towards a New Art, Painting 1910-20*, Tate Gallery Publications, London, 1980
P. Vogt, *The Blue Rider*, Barrons, Woodbury, 1980

Josef Albers (1888-1976)

German painter and designer, an important link between the European and American Abstract traditions. Albers was born in the Ruhr and trained as a teacher. He came late to art, studying under Von Stück (who had also taught Klee and Kandinsky) in 1919-20, and then joining the newly-formed Bauhaus as its oldest pupil. There, he produced a remarkable series of glass paintings and was offered a post as László Moholy-Nagy's assistant. Albers remained with the Bauhaus until its suppression by the Nazis in 1933, and then emigrated to the United States, where he taught at Black Mountain College, North Carolina, eventually becoming its Rector. His own artistic work was centred on the Homage to the Square series, in which the possibilities of colour relationships were explored through a single compositional form, that of squares set within squares. Albers explained his theories in his book The Interaction of Colour (1963) and these ideas have since become recognized as a corner-stone of Op Art.

Theo van Doesburg (1883-1931)

Dutch painter and writer, a leading member of the De Stijl group. Doesburg's early work was influenced by Kandinsky and the German Expressionists, but his style changed abruptly after he met Mondrian in 1915. Two years later, he was the driving force behind the foundation of De Stijl, an association of painters and architects dedicated to the creation of a new artistic language. Doesburg was the editor of the group's magazine, also called De Stijl, and much of his value to the circle was as a polemicist and organizer. In his paintings, he emulated the severe, geometric abstraction of Mondrian, although he occasionally introduced more dynamic elements. These are most obvious in his Contra-compositions, a series of works in which he used thrusting diagonals to off-set the rectangular shape of the picture. In 1930, just before he died, he issued the Manifesto of Concrete Art.

Auguste Herbin (1882-1960)

French painter, a co-founder of the Abstraction-Création group. Herbin's roots were in Cubism and, particularly, in Delaunay's colouristic version of the style. In 1931, he and Georges Vantongerloo set up Abstraction-Création, an important exhibiting body, which was intended to maintain the achievements of the Constructivist and De Stijl groups, while also countering the rise of Surrealism. Herbin's own experiments in relating geometric shapes to specific colours provided an important source of inspiration for the Op Artists.

El Lissitzky (Lazar) (1890-1941)

Russian painter and graphic artist. Lissitzky grew up in Smolensk but, owing to his Jewish background, he had to travel to Darmstadt to gain his education as an engineer and architect. During World War One, he was closely associated with Chagall and the avant-garde circles in Kiev and Vitebsk, producing book illustrations that drew heavily on Russian folk traditions. In 1919, the Tenth State Exhibition of abstract art introduced him to the ideas of the Suprematists, but Lissitzky rapidly adapted these to his own needs. His Prouns (meaning objects in Russian) were intended to constitute a purely functional form of painting and, as such, a synthesis of the Suprematist and Constructivist styles. During the 1920s, Lissitzky travelled extensively in Western Europe, becoming an important spokesman for the latest Russian developments.

Echaurren Roberto Matta (b.1912)

Chilean Surrealist painter. Matta trained in Santiago as an architect and, after his arrival in Paris in 1934, worked in Le Corbusier's studio. Through Dali, he gained an introduction to the Surrealist group and began producing his 'psychological morphologies', a series of swirling, biomorphic creations, resembling those of Miró and Tanguy. In 1939, Matta emigrated to the United States, where his work proved a significant influence on the Abstract Expressionists and, in particular, on Robert Motherwell and Arshile Gorky.

Piet Mondrian (1872-1944)

Major abstract artist, a leading figure in the De Stijl movement. Mondrian was born into a strict Calvinist family at Amersfoot, in Holland. His early development was extremely slow and he was in his mid thirties before he produced the Symbolist canvases that are his first masterpieces. In 1912 on a visit to Paris, Mondrian was overwhelmed by the discoveries of the Cubists and could not wait to return to France after the War. In the interim, however, he had become the pivotal figure in Van Doesburg's De Stijl movement, although he was eventually to withdraw from this to join the more astringent Abstraction-Création group. Mondrian defined his own style as 'Neo-Plasticism', which entailed the use of severe, geometric forms and a restricted palette, including only black, white and the primary colours. This austerity was only relieved after his departure for America, during World War Two, when his Broadway Boogie Woogie (1942-3, Museum of Modern Art, New York) – see opposite – captured something of the rhythm and energy of his new home.

Robert Motherwell (b. 1915)

American painter and writer, associated with both the Abstract Expressionists and the Surrealists. Motherwell studied philosophy at Harvard and did not become a full-time painter until 1941. Initially, he was drawn to the Surrealists, contributing to their New York show in 1939 and producing an important anthology of Dada painting and poetry, which appeared in 1951. In particular, he was fascinated by the Surrealists' use of automatic drawings and collages and, in his experiments with the latter, he worked in collaboration with Jackson Pollock. During the 1940s, he was closely linked with other Abstract Expressionists and, together with Newman and Rothko, he founded the 'Subjects of the Artist' school in 1948-9. Motherwell's own paintings exhibit a taste for grand, gestural effects and his best-known works are the series of Elegies to the Spanish Republic. From 1944 to 1957, he was editor of the influential Documents of Modern Art.

Lyubov Sergeevna Popova (1889-1924)
Russian artist and designer, linked with the Constructivists. Popova was born and studied in Moscow, but her education was completed by a trip to Paris in 1912, when she worked in the studios of Metzinger and Le Fauconnier. These artists from the Section d'Or group painted in a Cubo-Futurist style that had a profound influence on her early work. Returning to Russia at the outbreak of war, Popova exhibited with the 'Knave of Diamonds' circle. Gradually, she evolved an individual Constructivist manner, which culminated in the superb series of Architectonic Paintings in 1917-18. Like many of the Constructivists, however, Popova moved away from painting after the War and her last works included industrial designs for a textile factory and the creation of stage sets.

Alexander Mikhailovich Rodchenko (1891-1956)
Russian artist and designer, associated with the Constructivists. Rodchenko was born in St Petersburg and studied at the Kazan School of Art in Odessa. In 1914, he left this to join the School of Applied Arts in Moscow but here, as before, he failed to complete the course. His earliest paintings were influenced by Futurism, although this was rapidly superseded by an admiration for Malevich's work. However, in 1916, he contributed to the important exhibition which Tatlin organized in an empty Moscow shop. During the course of this show, Malevich quarrelled with Tatlin and Rodchenko sided with the latter. This fundamental breach was symbolized by his Black on Black (1918, Museum of Modern Art, New York), which he painted as a mischievous rebuttal of Malevich's White on White (p.67). Increasingly, Rodchenko grew disenchanted with easel paintings and concentrated on more utilitarian projects. His later work involved posters, photography and furniture design.

Nicolas de Staël (1914-55)
Gifted Russo-French painter, heir to the traditions of the School of Paris. De Staël was born in St Petersburg but grew up in Brussels, where he attended the Academy of Fine Arts. He travelled extensively during the 1930s but made his mark in the following decade, when he was working in close association with Braque. De Staël's abstract pictures were extremely sensual, employing rich colours and thickly applied brushstrokes. However, he felt increasingly that abstraction had reached an impasse and, in his later paintings, there was a return to figuration in which abstract forms resembled real objects. Tragically, de Staël committed suicide before the divisions in his style could be resolved.

Vladimir Tatlin (1885-1953)
Ukrainian painter and designer, a leading figure in the Constructivist movement. Tatlin began his working life as a sailor and many of his early drawing were on marine subjects. From 1911 to 1913, he was in close contact with Larionov and Goncharova, who introduced him to Russian folk art. Tatlin also admired the work of Cézanne, Picasso and – despite their bitter rivalry – Malevich. In 1913, he visited Paris, meeting Picasso, and, on his return, began the important series of Painting Reliefs. These were, effectively, three-dimensional versions of Cubist subjects and formed the basis for his radical Corner Reliefs. In common with other Revolutionary artists, Tatlin rejected fine art in favour of utilitarian projects, although ironically the two major schemes of his latter career proved thoroughly impractical and were never completed. These were the proposed Monument to the Third International and a man-powered glider called the Letatlin, which was based on his study of insects.

Victor Vasarély (b.1908)
Hungarian painter, a pioneer of Op Art. Vasarély studied medicine initially before turning to art and, in 1928, he entered the Budapest Bauhaus. Two years later, he moved to Paris, where he began work as a graphic artist. His first paintings date from 1943 and, by 1947, he was involved with pure abstraction. Formally, much of Vasarély's inspiration was drawn from the example of Auguste Herbin, who successfully integrated different geometric shapes, and he combined with this an interest in kinetic effects, through which sections of a painting would appear to advance or recede in the spectator's eye. Vasarély summarized his theories in his Yellow Manifesto of 1955.

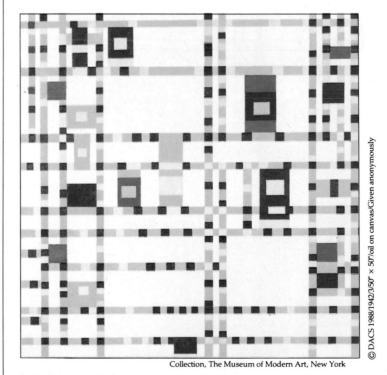

Collection, The Museum of Modern Art, New York

Broadway melody
(above) In Broadway Boogie Woogie, Mondrian embodied his love for jazz and the vigour of his new home.

INDEX